FRIENDSHIP ON FIRE

FRIENDSHIP ON FIRE

Passionate and Intimate Connections for Life

Dr. Linda Miles

Edited by: Dr. June Smart, Dr. Robert Miles

To order additional copies of this book, contact:
Xlibris Corporation
1-888-795-4274
www.Xlibris.com
Orders@Xlibris.com
46878

CONTENTS

FIRE OF SAFETY
CASE ILLUSTRATIONS

To my husband, Robert
My Friendship on Fire

Love is friendship set on fire.

—Jeremy Taylor

FRIENDSHIP ON FIRE

Someday, after we have mastered the winds, the waves, the tide and gravity, we shall harness for God, the energies of love. Then for the second time in the history of the world, man will have discovered fire.

—Teilhard de Chardin

Friendship on Fire

THE ENERGIES OF LOVE

Research has shown that people in loving and lasting unions are healthier, skinnier, have more frequent and better sex, make more money, and live longer.*

As a marriage and family therapist for over thirty years, I have lived the questions of how to manage the energies of love on a daily basis through my work with couples and in my own life.

When a gesture as simple as holding hands can calm stress hormones in the brain, imagine what a lifetime of love and connection can do for your health, happiness, and sense of well-being.

A GOOD RELATIONSHIP GIVES LIFE

My client Josie's parents were married for fifty years and still maintained a friendship on fire after four children and many life hurdles. As Josie's mother was dying, her father sat beside the bed and took his wife's hand. "Baby, it's OK to go. I will find you again." Following his words, she literally took her last breath. Josie was touched beyond words to see the affection between her parents.

The purpose of this book is to take you on my journey as a psychotherapist and illuminate a path in the direction of passionate and intimate connection for life. A good relationship gives life.

---

* p. 210.

Using many examples of clients I have seen over the years who maintained friendship on fire, I want to engender hope that you can sustain love. As I write on a lovely Fall afternoon, my intention is to reach out and touch your heart and mind by sharing what I have learned through professional and life experience.

FRIENDSHIP ON FIRE

What is a friendship on fire?

It is a compassionate and sensual bond that lasts because you find your soul's true home with your partner. The friendship offers safety, and the fire provides the sparks.

In a friendship on fire union, partners are advocates and protectors of the other and they share life-giving sparks of energy.

Robert Johnson observed that when we fall in love it is an initiation into spiritual forces much greater than ourselves. Friendship on fire is sustained by divine forces beyond our own egos. Those with this kind of lasting connection share the knowledge that love is what matters in life and make this a priority through gestures, facial expressions, touch, tone of voice; they are vigilant about the delicate connection of their souls. They remember that they are so much more than their egos.

Friendship on Fire is not for everyone. If you want a convenient partnership; blame others for your unhappiness, take your rage out on them or have addiction problems that you are not ready to face, this book is probably not for you. Friendship on Fire is about a shared life journey of souls.

Those with friendship on fire are guardians of each other's well-being.

Roberta and Burt maintained a friendship on fire for forty-five years. They laughed, declaring that they *had* to learn to work things out because the world felt too darn cold when they were at odds.

When Burt was dying of cancer, Roberta still saw the young man she first met. Although he weighed only ninety-five pounds and had an ashen color, she still felt their love. As he was dying on a Monday afternoon in the living room filled with memories, she expressed, "We have always worked things out together. I am with you now, and my love goes with you."

John Claypool wrote after the death of his eleven-year-old daughter, "For years, I took life for granted and assumed having a healthy family was precisely what I deserved. I see now what an astonishingly good fortune even a single day really is."

Learning to manage the tension between passionate expression and self-control opens the door to a friendship on fire. Years ago when our granddaughter, Merritt, was five, I was reading her a fairy tale and was disturbed by the ending "And they lived happily ever after."

So I took the liberty of changing the ending to, "They began the work of creating a very good marriage." I did not want Merritt thinking, as so many of my clients had, that marriage was so simple that it magically happened, and couples lived happily ever after.

I have seen the pain people experience after the honeymoon is over, when they awaken, realizing they have married a mere mortal. I hope to help you avoid the pitfalls of pain of those who succumb to the "happily every after" myth.

Those with friendship on fire live a reality tale based on living fully in the present moment. Dr. Norberto R. Keppe notes that ENVY causes many of our problems in relationships due to contamination of our thoughts by comparisons with others. These comparisons block our awareness of and gratitude for the abundance of goodness and beauty in others and the world around us. Friendship on fire is about connection and appreciation of one another and the abundance of grace that surrounds you.

LOOKING GOOD ON PAPER

I sat with a petite twenty-five-year-old with huge brown eyes who told me that she had learned that you cannot choose a partner simply because he has cool credentials. In her case, there was no fire with her handsome fiancé, an Ivy League med school student. When I asked her how she came to this conclusion, she shared that she had learned from her mother's divorce; her mother cautioned her to choose based on the real person and not because a guy looks good on paper. Friendship on fire combines the fire of strong feelings and a safe connection.

HOT IS NOT ENOUGH

I recall a mom who was very distressed when her seventeen-year-old daughter fell for a handsome and charming boy who sold drugs at school.

It turned out to be a great lesson for the teenager about what it was like with someone so undependable. *Hot was not enough.* Past relationships you consider failures may help prepare you for a friendship on fire.

Open your heart and mind to the daily practice of creating and maintaining a friendship on fire.

FUEL

This book is designed to provide fifty-two weeks of fuel for a friendship on fire. You can have a loving and lasting relationship, but it takes skill and preparation. It must include the three components of an enduring fire: spirit, connection, and safety. My couple clients taught me significant lessons that I want to share. Over the years I developed recommendations for new clients based on these lessons combined with study and research. These guidelines amplify ways to work with the material in this book:

- ➤ All there is is *now*. Focus on the present moment and current patterns. Do not worry about whether or not the old stuff will repeat.
- ➤ Use "we" statements to discuss what is in the best interest of both partners.
- ➤ Avoid "my way or the highway" verbiage.
- ➤ The brain loves the familiar, so look carefully at patterns you bring from your family of origin and how they become self-fulfilling prophesies.
- ➤ Do not do anything for your partner that he should do for himself so you do not help him stay stuck in immaturity.
- ➤ Alcohol can flambé a relationship. Avoid arguments when under the influence of drugs or alcohol.
- ➤ Make your relationship a safe place to be deeply honest with one another. Postpone discussion of differences if either of you becomes destructive. Take time-outs.
- ➤ Develop a toolbox of ways to calm down (e.g., prayer, meditation, exercise, music, etc.).
- ➤ Develop a toolbox of constructive communication techniques and avoid criticism, contempt, defensiveness, or stonewalling.
- ➤ Remember, you are not a cupcake and need to be open to feedback about distasteful habits.

➤ Both partners play a part in a destructive dance. It usually backfires to assign blame to your partner and ask friends and family to don a black robe and become judges.

➤ Right-wrong games are counterproductive since no judge drops out of the sky to declare a winner.

➤ Be open to your partner's point of view and negotiate instead of acting like two opposing attorneys making their cases.

➤ If your goal is to be on the same team, it is not helpful to hit one another over the head with words, and physical hitting is illegal.

➤ Be flexible about change, and let go of rigid patterns that never worked from day one. Do not keep buying a ticket to reruns of destructive dramas.

➤ Develop a positive emotional bank account by declaring one thing you appreciate about one another at the end of each day. These add up, and when you make withdrawals during bad times, you maintain a positive balance in the bank.

➤ Techniques like the ones presented in this book are meant to be practiced with hearts and smarts. If you apply only smarts, tools designed to be helpful can be spin-doctored into destructive barbs. For example, "We need to work on this together" can be spun into "We need to work on this together if you can stop being so selfish."

➤ Soul food is nourishing to relationships. Spiritual practices help open our hearts and minds to love.

➤ Choose love instead of fear to motivate your life.

➤ When you expect certain behavior from your partner, you may unconsciously provoke it. Say you walk in and your husband is frowning, so you think he does not care about seeing you and you mouth off. Better to ask if there is anything bothering him before you jump to conclusions.

➤ Since much of what you see comes from your own mind, you have choices about where to focus your attention. Look for the grace that surrounds you everyday.

➤ If you grew up with destructive patterns like alcoholism or abuse, you may overlook warning signs because the patterns are so familiar. Memorize the warning signs so you do not go on autopilot and repeat the past.

➤ Choose peace of mind instead of attack thoughts.

➤ Problems that are repetitive and difficult have roots in the past. For example, if you do not have self-confidence, you may think things like, "If he thought I was worth it, he would call" or "Since I disappointed her, she thinks I am a bad husband."

➤ Repetitive arguments are clues to unresolved problems in our memory that keep popping up. Pay attention. You can help one another heal.

➤ Remember that you are dealing with your partner's self-esteem. Be careful. How we are viewed by family and significant others is a vital part of our identity.

➤ Be careful what you believe about relationships. Our mind can work like a magnet to confirm our belief systems. I am amazed how many people see only the negative behaviors of their partners. I once saw a couple, and the man said repeatedly, "I love you and want to make this work." When I asked her what she heard, she insisted that he never said it.

➤ Do not take yourself too seriously. We all have flaws and, therefore, should avoid becoming too full of ourselves.

➤ Would you walk in a bar and go up to a brawny stranger, stare him in the eye, and offer the challenge, "What's with you?" Many partners issue such a challenge and then expect a warm, fuzzy response. Act the way you want to be treated.

➤ When your partner attacks or withdraws, it is often a cry for help even though they have a funny way of showing it. Couples do better if they can join one another in the pain and learn to ask for help.

➤ Many people are living with an elephant in the living room that they pretend is not there. That elephant can do a lot of damage if left unattended.

➤ Couples often say they have tried "everything" when in fact they have remained stuck in a few of the same rigid patterns.

➤ You can learn how to maintain a good relationship. This is the best gift you can give your children.

These are comments from couples who began with despair and learned how to repair their relationships:

"The areas that were scariest and hardest to work out turned out to be the very ones that helped us to grow, and once we dealt with them it was so freeing!"

"Although my perception is my reality, it is not necessarily the reality or situation of my partner."

"There is power and strength in gentleness, tenderness, and understanding of one another."

"Making a difficult but conscious choice at the moment of aggravation to step back, cool off, and not lose sight of the other person who is also hurting made the difference for us."

"We had another ceremony to begin our new marriage and let go of the old one after ten years."

"I wish everyone could feel what it is like to be in love again after eighteen years. I remember why I fell in love with him."

START WHERE YOU ARE

You do not need to do the readings in order although it is best to begin a regular practice of reading a section and doing the "Your Turn" exercises. Think of this as devoting time every week or two to enhance your relationship.

Start with the sections that speak to you . . . start where you are. Since this book is based on commonly occurring problems in relationships, rest assured that you are not alone. I have watched countless couples breathe a sigh of relief as this registers: "You mean, this is not just us!"

RIGHT HERE, RIGHT NOW

As a seasoned psychotherapist, I have learned that it is often necessary to throw my advance preparation out the window because my clients specify exactly what they need during that session. I have learned to ask them what they need most at that time. With the "right here, right now" lesson in mind, I begin this friendship-on-fire journey with a questionnaire designed to identify your current issues and direct you to applicable sections of the book.

Friendship On Fire Questionnaire

This book is designed to give you fuel for a loving and lasting relationship. Complete the following questionnaire to identify priority areas for your relationship. When you finish the questions, you will find references to page numbers that address the issues that you have identified.

In an ideal world, you might take a week for each section of the book and spend a year thinking about and discussing the "Your Turn" responses; however, chances are you will be interrupted. Start with what is most important, and return to other sections later.

Answer "true" or "false" for the following questions. You may take this if you are alone or currently in a relationship. Answer what is most true for you at this time in your life. Regarding question 1, for example, you may feel isolated and lonely when you are with your current partner as much as or more than someone who does not have a partner. Regarding question 2, even if you are not in a relationship now, you may have had problems in the past with intolerance. This list features problems that couples frequently report, so you are not alone. The questions will help you to identify and attack the problems and not one another.

QUESTIONNAIRE

1. I feel isolated and lonely.
2. I am intolerant of my partner.
3. I resent my partner.
4. I lash out at my partner.
5. My partner lashes out at me.
6. Sex is a major problem for us.
7. I use criticism too often.
8. My partner uses criticism too often.
9. I have lost respect for my partner.
10. My partner has lost respect for me.
11. We avoid dealing with conflicts.
12. We need to learn how to fight fair.
13. Our life together is boring.
14. My life is too stressful.
15. I experience very little joy.
16. I feel as if I have lost track of who I am.
17. I have recently experienced a death in the immediate family.
18. I feel anxious a lot.
19. I feel a sense of emptiness.
20. I wish I could laugh more often.
21. We do not work well as a team.
22. We do not support one another when we are dealing with the children.
23. I experience a lack of purpose in my life.
24. I worry a lot.
25. My partner and I have lost our connection.
26. We have a hard time understanding one another.
27. I have lost trust in my partner.
28. My partner has lost trust in me.
29. I keep my unhappiness inside and pretend that things are OK.
30. I have felt depressed for more than a month.
31. I have a problem with drinking or drugs.
32. My partner has a problem with drinking or drugs.
33. I put myself down too much.
34. I feel like I always have to be the grown-up.
35. I wish we had a spiritual practice.

KINDLE YOUR KNOWLEDGE

As you work on your relationship, your ability to sustain friendship on fire will increase. "Knowledge always demands increase; it is like fire which must first be kindled by some external agent, but will afterwards always propagate itself" (Samuel Johnson).

If you have a lot of "true" answers, remember that you have lots of company—these are all common relationship problems. When more of us fire our minds with the passionate belief that our families can live by love, we spread light for others.

Flip to the appendix in the back of the book for a handy questionnaire page reference guide. Once you determine which questions represent problem areas in your friendship on fire, helpful exercises and inspiring passages will be right at your fingertips.

The APPENDIX found on page 215 provides a guide for dealing with your specific problem areas. Try out some of the strategies and set your intention for a loving and lasting union.

After the Questionnaire: Summary

PRIORITIES

Go back over the questions that you answered "true" and mark your ten highest priorities. Locate the sections of the book that deal with your specific challenges. These are the sections that are likely to be the most relevant to you now.

My suggestion is that you think of this book as a weekly commitment to improve yourself and your relationship. Try to devote a time to problem solving in each area that you have chosen, and then choose the next ten priorities.

There is no right way to use this. You may prefer to skim through the sections first and then make choices. This book is designed to be flexible and to steer you toward friendship on fire.

Friendship on fire is not about perfect relationships; it is a reality tale and not a fairy tale. The case examples are brief and cannot do justice to the work that couples do to maintain passion and friendship over time. They make mistakes and drift off course but learn the lessons of loving, repair, and steer toward a passion for everyday living.

Learning to manage the tension between passionate expression and self-control opens the door to a friendship on fire.

The book is divided into sections under three headings: "Fire of Spirit," "Fire of Connection," and "Fire of Safety."

FIRE OF SPIRIT

Fire of spirit begins with a focus on your inner life, since you need self-awareness to sustain friendship on fire. You hold the matches.

Awareness practices help you to stay centered. You must be able to detach and calm yourself if you want to maintain friendship on fire.

Logs of Self-Loathing

Self-hatred interferes with deep and authentic connections with others. Logs of self-loathing can fuel destructive internal fires and consume your energy and you may focus on envy instead of opening to joy and love. The first sections of the book will help you to set aside self-loathing and enkindle your fire of spirit.

Spiritual Being

The fire of spirit case examples teaches how to observe your thoughts through awareness practices. You are not your thoughts. You are a spiritual being having a human experience.

The fire of spirit cases are about waking up. Spiritual practices help you to stop thinking so much with your ego and listen for the messages from your soul.

FIRE OF CONNECTION

The "Fire of Connection" section focuses on the connection between you and your partner. A philosopher and priest, Teilhard de Chardin, performed a wedding and explained that there were three entities that were getting married: the bride, groom, and the marriage itself. He described the marriage as a baby and cautioned that if the baby is not cared for, it will get sick and die.

Fire of connection is about caring for the baby. If couples are mired in shame and blame, they neglect the third entity.

FIRE OF SAFETY

Fire of safety cases deal with threats to friendship on fire and how to foster peace and security in your relationship.

Choose Your Relationship as if Your Life Depends on It

Shakespeare once wrote, "There is no safety but in risking all for love." Since research has shown that those with loving and lasting unions are healthier, skinnier, have more frequent and better sex, make more money, and live longer, choose your partner as if your life depends on it.

How do you protect one another and the relationship? Those with friendship on fire are experts at controlled burns.

Controlled Burns

As I write this on the Fourth of July, I can hear fireworks all around me as a reminder of the wild surprises of passion. On the other hand, some of the worst wildfires in a decade are blazing out of control in California. I am reminded that passion can also become wildfire, destructive and all-consuming. You need a well-established friendship so that the fire will only consume what it should. In this way, the relationship (like the forest) can be cleansed of combustible debris and nourished.

Everyone is aware of fire's potential to warm and comfort or destroy. Forest rangers use controlled burns to rid the forest of underbrush and keep it healthy. There was a time when the forest service attempted to put out every blaze, no matter how small, as soon as possible. In recent years, they have realized that simply containing the fires is better for the forest.

They are also aware, of course, that a fire should not burn unrestricted and cause harm to the fragile ecosystem—plants, animals, soil, water, and air. It must be controlled, preserving the ecosystem while ridding it of deadwood and thick underbrush that might ignite dangerously.

While the heat from a controlled burn is just as intense as a wildfire, it is contained within boundaries. So is it with a loving and lasting relationship. The passion essential to keeping a relationship alive is managed within the safety of friendship.

THE COMPONENTS OF FRIENDSHIP ON FIRE

- ➤ Sparks your connection so you cannot walk away without a huge loss of warmth
- ➤ Gives energy and life
- ➤ Provides the energy to burn off underbrush and grow
- ➤ Connects you to the spark of the divine

FRIENDSHIP

- ➤ Provides safety
- ➤ Gives compassion and encouragement to live true purpose
- ➤ Develops skills for controlled burns and conflict management
- ➤ Offers mutual commitment to health, happiness, and spiritual growth

Friendship-on-fire couples repair conflicts in a timely way. They use friendship skills like compassion and respect to set controlled burns. They do not let bad feelings smolder. Holding on to anger is like holding a hot charcoal briquette in your hand with the intention of throwing it at your partner. *You* get burned.

By illuminating and dealing with your differences, you let go of the past. A controlled burn brings forgiveness while releasing anger and grief.

So check your page numbers, commit to some time, and light the torch for a friendship on fire.

FIRE OF SPIRIT

*Love partakes of the soul itself. It is of the same nature. Like the soul,
it is a divine spark . . . it is a point of fire within us.*

—Victor Hugo

Introduction
To Fire Of Spirit

PULLING TOGETHER

Two dear friends, Jinmi and Nick Huseman, epitomize the friendship-on-fire spirit in the midst of one of the worst tragedies: the loss of their seven-month-old baby, Rece Nicholas Huseman, as a result of SIDS in 2008. They want to share their experience of facing this loss together in honor of Rece.

When I asked them what they learned about one another and life as a result of this crisis, they answered,

> We became aware of the depth of one another as spiritual beings. Six weeks after losing Rece, our spiritual journey led us to new perspectives of the cycle of life . . . We had to get away from all the outside influences (other people brought an element of toxicity that distracted us from coping). It was a physical act of pulling together and paving our path. We are partners in life. Even when we oscillate at different currents of emotion, we know we are in this together.

LEVEL OF COMMITMENT

In my practice, I observed that it was not the difficulty of the circumstances that pulled couples apart; rather, it was their lack of commitment to one another and inability to be partners in life.

Research shows that couples who develop spiritual practices like Jinmi and Nick are better able to weather the vicissitudes of life

LOVE PARTAKES OF THE SOUL

Love is an expression of our spirit. It is the fuel that moves our souls. As the Talmud tells us, "God wants your heart." The Greek word *enthousiasmos* referred to a god within and the word enthusiasm, derived from the Greek can be thought of as faith set on fire. Approach these sections with enthusiasm for the intention to abide in love.

The "Fire of Spirit" section helps you:

- ➤ express your deep, authentic self;
- ➤ develop spiritual practices to transcend your ego;
- ➤ find a calm and peaceful place within yourself;
- ➤ celebrate every day;
- ➤ spark your inner happiness;
- ➤ take time out to center before saying or doing destructive things;
- ➤ identify inner firetraps;
- ➤ live in the moment;
- ➤ choose peace of mind instead of attack thoughts;
- ➤ develop constructive and creative outlets;
- ➤ accept what is;
- ➤ stop blaming and start living;
- ➤ use the matches in your hand in life-giving ways;
- ➤ refrain from setting damaging fires;
- ➤ seek inspiration, wisdom, and positive models for relationships;
- ➤ unite the fire of passion with the sacred path that connects you to a higher reality of the spirit;
- ➤ allow negative feelings to flow through you without becoming attached;
- ➤ deal with grief; and
- ➤ invite the presence of God.

"The marriage becomes a witness to God's desire to be among us as a faithful friend" (Henri Nouwen). In order to maintain friendship on fire, you need to face your own opinion or sense of yourself. When I hear the expression, "You are too full of yourself," I am reminded that when the ego is too full of inaccurate notions about self-worth based on past programming that there is little room for God. Envy rules your thoughts and you are blocked from the bounty of the present moment,

We are so much more than our programmed thoughts. A lasting bond that survives hardship calls for you to face your fear that you are defective and inadequate and realize that you are so much more than you think you are.

Jinmi and Nick refrained from shame and blame, transcended their egos, and pulled together to face this tragedy and share a spiritual journey.

You are much bigger than your *ego*.

To live friendship on fire, you need to be able to go inside yourself and break free of the limitations of ego programming so you can connect to your partner from your spacious higher self. Fire of spirit helps you learn to find your own center and create a spiritual journey that you can share with your partner.

Firetraps in Your Mind

Hillary came for her first appointment wearing a peasant dress and drinking bottled water. Despite her bouncy entrance, it was clear that she looked fatigued and troubled.

PUT DOWN

She reported that she had not been sleeping well and was troubled by a recurrent dream. In the dream, she is trapped in her basement with weird creatures that fill her with fear and dread. An old lady owns the house and keeps her as a prisoner in the basement with the creatures.

I responded by telling her that her dream was encouraging, as her unconscious was bringing unresolved fears to her attention. She put down her bottled water, rolled her eyes, and looked at me skeptically.

I explained that our unconscious aims to protect us, and that conflict may come to the surface in dream images. As we discussed the dream, she realized that she did feel trapped by the need for approval from the important women in her life: her mother and her elder sister. Although she gave a good imitation of a free spirit, inside, she was filled with guilt and self-doubts.

She had felt "put down" by these women, and the creatures in the basement reflected patterns and thoughts related to a prison of her own ideas. Her tendency to put herself down caused her to be overly jealous and controlling of her husband. She watched him like a hawk instead of turning her attention to her inner conflict.

NEXT

Together, we devised a plan for her to break out of the basement. We called the practice NEXT to indicate that there were new and different ways of being.

N stands for "I am NOT only my thoughts." I recommended that Hillary think of herself as a spiritual being having a human experience. As we developed a practice of awareness based on the principles in this book, she was able to get in touch with her higher wisdom and became less judgmental of herself and others. As she gained valuable perspective about the mean-spirited thoughts and could watch them pass through her mind the mean-spirited creatures disappeared from her dreams.

E stands for ENVY. As Hillary got in touch with her deepest values she learned to choose love instead of envy . . . . compassion instead of attack thoughts. She realized how often her thoughts were about envy and comparisons to others. She worked on acceptance and empathy for herself and others and began to live in the present moment. As she realized that she was trapped by her own judgmental thoughts the basement dreams stopped.

X stands for "X marks the spot." Hillary learned to feel the tightness, guilt and fear in her body when she envied others. She stopped playing out daily dramas and began to notice how she repeated mean-spirited patterns in her own mind. She no longer needed unconscious reminders from her dreams once she broke out of the basement of her own ideas. Through daily awareness she realized how conflicts began and ended with HER.

T stands for TRANSFORMATION. Over a period of years, Hillary began to transform her thinking and open the door to new possibilities. As her thinking expanded, she became more creative and flexible. Without the noise of guilt and envy in her mind, she heard the voice of her Higher Wisdom.

EAT, PRAY, LIVE

Elizabeth Gilbert does a beautiful job of describing transformation in her popular book *Eat, Pray, Love* when the voice of Higher Wisdom, roared,

"YOU HAVE NO IDEA HOW STRONG MY LOVE IS!!!!"

The chattering, negative thoughts in my mind scattered in the wind of this statement like birds and jackrabbits and antelopes—they hightailed it out of there, terrified. Silence followed . . . and then, in that regal silence, finally—I began to meditate on (and with) God."

Hillary scattered the creatures in her basement dreams in much the same way and realized that when she let go of envy, the love of God could shine into her inner darkness. I use these strategies in my own life. When I feel tense and conflicted around someone I refocus on MY thinking and examine my inner fracas. In brief the process goes:

> N/ I am NOT these chattering negative thoughts.
> E/ Who or what do I ENVY that blocks my gratitude for the grace of the present moment?
> X/X Marks the spot of tension in my body that warns of negative thoughts that I need to deal with.
> T/ I observe the negative thoughts and center my attention on TRANFORMATION and Higher Wisdom.

The following chapters will provide many ways to use the NEXT model helping you live in a conscious and loving way . . . from next moment to next moment . . .

SPIRITUAL PRACTICE

The practices in this book are devoted to kindness and love. As Padre Pio once said, "If prayer does not lead to love, it is not prayer." The spiritual practices in this book help you

> ➢ live in the here and now,
> ➢ remain peaceful and centered,
> ➢ remain connected to the sacred in everyday life,
> ➢ release energy for loving, and
> ➢ Strengthen your connection with your partner and to the divine.

Many practices will be presented in the "Fire of Spirit" section. Pick the ones that work best to help you transcend your ego and experience the sacred. For some, the goal will be simply to remain calm and centered in the present moment. Start where you are.

CENTERING PRAYER

A spiritual practice that brings acceptance and gratitude is the centering prayer, a meditative prayer developed by Father Thomas Keating.

Choose a sacred word that expresses your intention to sit and consent to the presence of God. You can choose names like Christ, God, Father, etc.; or you can use qualities such as love, compassion, kindness.

- Silently repeat the word as an invitation for God's presence in your life.
- If your thoughts wander, that is fine. Notice the thought and return to the sacred word.
- You are training your brain to center in peace and prayer.
- When thoughts wander, notice and redirect your attention to your sacred word.
- Open your heart and mind to receive divine direction.

Practice deep breathing and centering to calm yourself. Your mind may want to race in many directions. You may imagine you are like a television satellite that can tune into hundreds of stations, yet by repeating your sacred word, you learn to focus on a station that inspires and heals you and your relationships. This will help you stay centered in peace and loving intention as you encounter the passionate wheels of fire in a deeply loving union.

June Carter wrote a famous song for her husband, musician Johnny Cash, which goes, "We fell into a burning ring of fire—and it burns, burns, burns." June was able to stay centered in her values as she and her family helped support Johnny during his recovery from drug abuse.

A friendship on fire begins with YOU and your ability to choose love instead of attack thoughts.

Fireworks

Twenty-nine-year-old Kate took great pride in her trigger-happy, hostile approach to arguments. She was indeed a wordsmith and could cut to the bone. She was good at being bad.

HANGDOG HOARDING

Her boyfriend, Jim, maintained a hangdog look while his mind raced to the moon when Kate began to yammer and accumulated negative feelings. I have seen many clients who accumulate hangdog moments and hurt until they reach a surge point and either pack their bags to escape to higher ground or explode with aggression and reel off details of long-gone grievances.

While Jim was stuck in hangdog mode, Kate mistakenly concluded her aggressiveness worked, and it helped him listen if she became even more hyped up and yelled louder. Jim's mind headed for another galaxy at warp speed.

WIN THE BATTLES BUT LOSE THE WAR

When Jim announced that he wanted to break up, Kate was devastated because she loved the guy. He snapped back, "You might have won the battles, Kate, but you sure lost the war."

Although it was too late to repair this relationship, Kate remained in therapy to work on the behavior that she once thought was her crowning glory. She had to learn to stop throwing her trigger-happy barbs at those she cared for most. Her quick wit was her strength in many ways, but it backfired with Jim. She needed to learn to think through her words and avoid put-downs.

BE STRONG, NOT MEAN

Kate confused being strong with being mean. In my practice, I have found many people believe they need to say and do cruel things to show strength.

Friendship on fire couples know they need to take a time-out rather than argue if they are too upset to deal rationally with a problem. Words spoken in a heated moment can cut to the bone with hurt and guilt festering for years. Sticks and stones may break your bones, but words can break your soul.

STICKS AND STONES

While doing a speech at a bookstore, I pointed out that physical wounds usually heal while emotional wounds may resonate for years. A talented young songwriter, Sarah Rogers, was in the audience and later wrote a song about this theme entitled "Sticks and Stones May Break My Bones, but Words Can Break My Soul."

MAKEUP SEX

Resolving differences in a calmer manner finds its rewards in hot and heavy stuff in the bedroom. Makeup sex generates countless positive rewards, including chemicals whizzing around that help heal the mind and body. Remember: sex after resolving a fight is hot, but unresolved anger will burn you both.

BIRDBRAINED BEHAVIORS

When we are upset, we activate the primitive parts of our brain that we have in common with reptiles and birds, hence the term "birdbrained." So if you don't want to sound like a birdbrain, take time to cool off before you fight, freeze, or flee in a wrongheaded way.

TELL THE TRUTH WITH LOVE

Kate's pride in her viper tongue diminished as she lived and learned the consequences of quick, sharp words. Those with *friendship on fire* know how to tell the truth with love. Kate began spiritual practices to transform aggression into compassion. She channeled her strength through love and generated more of her zippy, positive chemicals. She learned a tough lesson about love from her breakup, but she was able to forgive herself for repeating a behavior that had protected her as the youngest and only girl with four older brothers. It served her then to have a mouth on her, and the family thought it was cute.

"OUR" SUFFERING

If you are in a relationship that helps keep you stuck in destructive patterns, you have loads of company. If you think in terms of "our" suffering instead of "my" suffering, it would help to motivate you to repair your mistakes and build a better world.

Your Turn

Do you and your partner have ways to sit and talk and repair differences without hissing and showing your fangs? Do you use snaky stares or viper tongues when you argue? If the answer is yes, talk about how you can discuss things in a calm and firm way when you have inevitable differences. Work out a signal that you need a time-out to refrain from saying birdbrained things or showing your fangs.

When you are too upset to discuss things, use a relaxation exercise before you deal with the problem. It will help you feel more centered. Guided imagery helps you refocus away from threatening thoughts, reduces the flow of negative hormones, may lower blood pressure, helps strengthen your immune system's ability to handle stress, and improves sleep. With all these positive things going for it, how can you pass this one up?

A method called progressive relaxation developed by Dr. Edmund Jacobson works well. Here are the instructions:

- Lie down in a comfortable position.
- Close your eyes.
- Breathe slowly and deeply as you count to seven in your mind.

- Let your attention focus on your body. Feel the pressure of your back, legs, buttocks, shoulders, and head against the surface you are lying on.
- Focus your attention on your feet and toes. Release the muscles in your toes and feet; allow them to relax.
- Notice your legs against the surface where you are lying. Allow the muscles in your legs to let go and relax.
- Focus your attention on your buttocks and lower back. Relax those muscles. No rush. No hurry.
- Relax the muscles in your belly. Become aware of the tension you hold there. Let it go.
- Focus on your shoulders and upper back. Feel any tension you are holding, and relax those muscles.
- Focus on the tension you hold in your chest and neck. Let the muscles relax. You may breathe more deeply. You may feel heavier in a pleasant way.
- Imagine the tension flowing down your arms and out of your fingers. Allow the tension to flow out of your body, giving you a pleasant sensation of relaxation.
- Notice the muscles in your face. Release the tension. Release tension in your mouth; unclench your teeth. Relax the muscles of your eyes.
- Let the muscles in your face become slack. Listen to your breathing. You may be breathing more deeply, feeling a pleasant sensation of relaxation.
- Lie there for a few minutes, allowing excess tension to flow from your fingers, attending to your breath and feeling a pleasant sense of relaxation.

Feel free to make your own adjustments.

MOVING OUT OF YOUR EGO

Another useful practice is a form of yoga taught by Pema Chödrön. This work was central to Kate's healing.

After you are in a relaxed state, breathe in to allow your body to open up to negative emotions such as anger, fear, or hurt. Create a space within yourself to make room for the negative emotions. Think of the pain as ain" to remind you of how many other beings share these emotions at this moment in time. As you breathe out, imagine that you breathe out healing to yourself and all others who are struggling with similar emotions as you begin to experience the human condition and radiate healing.

This practice helps you deal with emotions and realize that emotions are universal, that it really is "our" pain. As you move away from your ego, it is easier to face mistakes—yours and others'—and offer forgiveness.

The practice of breathing in your painful emotions and breathing out healing for self and others allows you to make space for pain and the vision of hope.

When we accept pain rather than resist, our energy can move toward healing ourselves and others. In order to maintain friendship on fire, we need to create the spaciousness inside to transcend our ego and use higher wisdom to help heal one another. This practice helps you move from ego attack when you feel small and isolated toward unfathomable spirit and loving connection.

Happiness Starts with Spark

Do not seek perfection in a changing world. Instead perfect your love.
—Master Sengstan

Charlotte, a fifty-year-old housewife recovering from anxiety, described how good it felt to get a big whiff of the grass in her yard. Like many people who experience anxiety or panic, Charlotte could not enjoy the world around her. She often focused on fearful thoughts, which made things seem worse than they really were.

QUIET THE BEEHIVE IN YOUR HEAD

Small problems became huge and out of proportion to reality. The day when a small thing, like enjoying the smell of fresh cut grass, made the world real, she felt happy. Charlotte had begun to learn how to quiet the beehive in her head and live in the present. She became aware that she had stopped smelling the grass as a teenager when she had her first bout with anxiety.

Charlotte's life changed as she learned to become aware of her surroundings and live in the present moment, and began to appreciate the small things in her life. She began taking yoga, listening to calm music, and learning meditation.

AWAKEN TO THE WORLD AROUND YOU

When she enjoyed the smell of freshly mowed grass, she knew she was getting better. She was able to shift her focus away from fear and self-doubt to reaching out to the world around her. Her inner world was filled with toxic gas made of past mistakes and future fears.

CENTERING IN THE PRESENT MOMENT

As Charlotte learned to remain centered in the present moment much of the time, she was able to reconnect with her husband. She needed internal freedom in order to move from ego to essence. "Feeling that we are continually falling short is like a toxic gas we breathe, making it difficult to be truly intimate with others and at home in our body, mind and heart" (Tara Brach).

"OUT OF YOUR MIND AND INTO YOUR SENSES"

Awareness practice allows you to focus on the present moment and fully experience what is happening in your life. Dr. Fritz Perls referred to this as "getting out of your mind and into your senses."

Unfortunately, many people are unaware that they walk around in a state of fear and, therefore, live in the past or future. It is difficult to maintain a *friendship on fire* if you are not able to experience the present. You also need a practice that helps you stay peaceful and centered so you can travel away from the rooms in your mind that are filled with toxic fumes of guilt and fear.

THE SONG OF YOUR SOUL

Begin a practice of awareness. Focus your attention on simple everyday things and become fully present.

> Most minds do not live in the present. Most minds abruptly turn
> and undermine the chance of humming. (Rumi)

Keep focusing your mind on the humming of life around you and away from conditioned reactions. If you train your mind to tune into the hum of life, you tune out the beehive of negative thoughts. Hum the song of your soul.

When you develop a deliberate practice, you can smell, touch, and really experience the moment.

In the depth of winter I finally learned there was within me an invincible summer. (Albert Camus)

Your Turn

Take a moment and look around your house or yard. What draws your attention? Focus on an object or person. Look at it as you never have before, look for details, and ask yourself what you really see. For example, you may see a plant and allow your consciousness to focus on the color green and the lustrous leaves or their shapes. See what you see, hear what you hear, smell what you smell, and touch what you touch. Bring your awareness into your senses.

Try a walking practice for a few minutes, allowing your attention to remain focused on the experience of nature around you. Your mind may wander, but that is OK. Redirect your attention to what you see, hear, feel, touch. A practice of awareness is like training a puppy. You keep bringing your attention back from distractions. You notice a wandering thought then redirect attention through your senses. Train your brain to relax and enjoy the world around you.

You will find that this focus brings a deeper experience of the moment, and these moments build into a practice of awareness. You might also want to repeat a phrase such as "Be calm." Say the word "be" as you breathe in and "calm" as you breathe out. Replace your beehive brain with the peace of mind that comes with surrendering to the moment.

How can you be more aware of the touch, smell, looks, and feelings that you have when you are with your partner? Think about how you could increase awareness as a couple. By developing your senses for things around you in the natural world, your senses can expand toward feelings for yourself and others in the present moment.

A friendship on fire is possible when you learn to calm yourself, live in the present moment, and accept faults in yourself and your partner.

Stay Away
From The Pizza Oven

Melissa explained to her husband, Tony, that for more than ten years, she didn't feel heard, or understood. She would sometimes shout, "You just don't get me." She repeatedly told him, "You just don't listen! You never take my needs into consideration when you are making important decisions about our relationship, our home, or in so many little things. I feel invisible."

For Melissa, the last straw was a pizza. Their relationship ended the night Tony ordered a pizza with all anchovies. Melissa hated anchovies. She looked across the table at Tony and calmly told him, "Tony, this is the last pizza you will ever order for me! I am leaving."

Tony was shocked; he thought Melissa was happy. In reality, he was oblivious to Melissa's needs. He just took it for granted that regardless of how he acted, Melissa would be there. For Melissa, the pizza man had been circling the neighborhood for quite some time; but on that night, he made a delivery.

A simple act can trigger an avalanche of past feelings; you decide you can no longer accept what is happening. You build a rock pile over time, and with one last rock, it tumbles.

How do you avoid the pizza man? You listen to your partner. By failing to listen, you are making a statement that you are indifferent to his/her feelings. They don't matter in your scheme of things. Having listened, you can address things that bother you, repair damage in a timely way, and discuss what is happening and how and why you feel the way you do. When we hurt one another with words or actions, the damage adds up.

In over thirty years of practice as a psychotherapist, I have seen many pizza-man scenarios. If you think your relationship may be heading in the wrong direction, work on things together before you get a delivery.

Recently, a client called me from the parking lot at the grocery store and left a message, "I had to get away and give you a call because the pizza man is in my neighborhood." She knew they needed a time-out.

Do not let damage accumulate in your relationship. Work together to repair hurts in a timely way. If a lot of damage has accumulated, you may want to seek therapy to help sort through the issues.

Charlotte Beck points out that when we focus our awareness on problems, it can be like a flame that burns through egocentric confusion. But when our attention is scattered, we make messes out of situations like burning soft coal that scatters soot all around.

Your Turn

If the pizza man is in your neighborhood, act now to repair your relationship while feelings are still strong. When the pizza man knocks on your door, it will be too late.

Ask yourself the following questions, and be ready to address them with one another in a nonthreatening, non-accusatory way.

1. What are the things that bother you on an ongoing basis in relationship?
2. Do you deal with issues on an ongoing basis? (Strike when the iron is cold. Deal with problems when things are calm between you and your partner, and take time off if things become too heated.)
3. How can you tell the truth with love more often?
4. Can you make an agreement to take a time-out if things become too heated between you and your partner? (Some couples develop a head signal or a phrase like, "We know where this ends.") It is important to acknowledge your partner's request for time-out, but you also need to deal with the issue later after things calm down.
5. How can you use some of the strategies in this book to calm yourselves down?

6. Do you often avoid dealing with issues that trouble you? How can you agree as a couple to begin to address these through controlled burns, burning off underbrush without damaging the roots of your relationship?

7. What are some things you need to accept about your partner? Do you expect him to morph into a different person (e.g., you may be a detail person and your partner may be a big-picture person)?

8. How can you work as a team to accept the differences of your partner and build on your combined strengths (e.g., you do details and your partner plans for social events)?

Ego Eruptions

Ninety-five percent of Americans report that they want a loving and lasting relationship, but because of the way they think, many people are convinced they can never have a *friendship on fire*. Aside from a few die-hard misanthropes, nearly everyone wants a loving and lasting relationship, but so many are hampered by a negative mindset that will not permit them to believe that they can enjoy a *friendship on fire*. They can't believe in themselves. If you want to sustain a loving and lasting relationship, you need to be a friend to yourself first.

Janet is thirty-seven, divorced, and her biological clock is racing. In her first therapy session, Janet sat slumped on the couch. She defined herself as a loser after her five-year relationship fell apart. Although she is an attractive and engaging woman, she had decided, "I will never have a successful relationship!" Her deep-seated conviction that she was bound to fail was paralyzing her.

SELF-IMPOSED SUFFERING

Why had the breakup of a relationship left her in such a state? For one thing, like many of my clients, most of Janet's suffering was about *her* and not the loss of the relationship. Her story was typical of many people who need to face self-imposed pain. She was not happy in the relationship and had thought of ending it herself many times, but when *he* dared to end it, an avalanche of murky self-doubts spilled out.

HOW MUCH OF THIS IS ME?

A good question to ask after a breakup is, "How much of my suffering is about *me*, and how much is about the loss of a super relationship?" Most of what I have heard over the years is super self-imposed suffering after a destructive relationship or self-recrimination from those who failed to appreciate a good one. They re-hash yesterday's news rather than learn the lessons and move on.

Many of my clients waste a lot of time with depressing inner judgments before beginning the practice of compassionate self-acceptance. They do not recognize that they walk around in a world covered with ash from their own ego eruptions blocking out God's loving light shining through the present moment.

HAZE OF SELF-DOUBT

Janet had let her mind become shrouded in a haze of self-doubt and a sense of unworthiness. Gnawed by a perpetual feeling of inadequacy, prone to magnify her faults, she was unable to see her way clearly toward self-acceptance. Having imposed such a dismal assessment upon herself, she could only conclude that the failure of the relationship was her fault. She felt downright worthless.

THE CALL OF LIFE

When you encounter people you regard as cool, popular, attractive, and capable of doing things you would like to do, you start comparing yourself to them. Inhibited by your sense of inadequacy and fearful of rejection, you hold back from being authentic and alive in the moment. You may be hampered by blinders that won't let you see beyond your own defects. Dr. Seuss may have had self-consciousness in mind when he urged us to jettison inhibitions and heed the call of life:

> Let us quit all this waiting and staying and go to the place where the boom band is playing.

For Janet, heeding the call of life meant entering a relationship with a guy of her choice. But she was so preoccupied with her own inadequacy she was convinced that any guy would see through the attractive self she tried to project and discover she was really defective.

Friendship on fire is about getting into your flow and being real. Janet's fear of discovery shrouded her sense of her own worth. She was unable to value herself and made choices dictated by her need for approval and acceptance by others. When this validation was not forthcoming and a relationship failed, she condemned herself and blamed her faults. Preoccupation with her faults became a blinding obsession, a dismal curtain that blocked her inner light.

Janet learned to recognize her smog of self-hatred during therapy through a mindfulness practice of self-acceptance and training her brain to refocus away from her negative programming and toward love and light.

Why did she make such self-defeating decisions that left her so vulnerable? She grew up comparing herself to others and became convinced at an early age that she must be defective. Through therapy, she learned how to jettison negative thought patterns, particularly the habit of self-condemnation. Morever, she learned to redirect her thoughts toward her loveable qualities and figure out how she could engage others with her true self rather than the faux self she had been projecting.

FALSE SELF

If you have become bogged down in self-condemnation as a result of early life decisions related to siblings, competition, disappointments in school, family conflict, or peer pressure, you have loads of company. Lots of people have wandered into the haze and lost touch with their true selves. Fearing that their defects will be discovered, they cling to faux selves and try to hide what they perceive as unacceptable inadequacies.

How do you know if your life is limited by a false self? Here are the symptoms:

- Going gonzo over fantasy folks like movie or pop stars
- Becoming tongue-tied as you search for the perfect thing to say
- Needing to remain as cool as a cucumber if you are attracted to someone
- Feeling mushy-headed in the presence of "cool" people
- Believing you don't deserve a person to whom you are attracted

- Thinking that if you are chosen for something, it has to be a mistake
- Walking into a crowded room wondering what everyone thinks of you instead of what you think of them
- Driven to distraction with the idea that you need to run before your chosen one discovers your defects
- Choosing to act "cool" instead of dancing

It takes courage to love and go for *friendship on fire*. You need to dump a lot of baggage filled with costumes and disguises and risk rejection. When your relationship is a *friendship on fire,* you are vulnerable yet safe. You come home to yourself and nourish the deep desire to be known and accepted.

DIVINE SPARK

The ancient Stoics believed that everyone had a spark of divinity within them. Early Christian writers baptized this idea, and it has been revived periodically through the centuries. Louis Pasteur observed, "The grandeur of the acts of men is measured by the inspiration from which they spring. Happy is he who bears a God within."

The divine spark of awareness within you can direct you in making authentic self-assessments, accepting your faults, and practicing loving kindness toward yourself and others.

"The most beautiful and profound emotion we can experience is the sensation of the mystical. It is the power of all science" (Albert Einstein). Janet lost touch with this inner experience.

When you become self-conscious and too vulnerable to the opinions of others, you lose touch with your center and higher self. You lose a sense of your own worth as a unique human being.

CLEARING YOUR MIND

The clarity of perspective is much like the first time you put on glasses to correct your vision. The first time I put on glasses in the doctor's office, I was surprised when I saw blades of grass instead of a green clump. With glasses, I could see what I had missed.

Awareness practice has the same effect. You learn to clear your mind so you can embrace the gifts of the present moment. When we are preoccupied with our own self-importance, we are unaware of the boundless gifts of God all around us.

"Everything has beauty, but not everyone sees it" (Confucius).

SOLUTIONS FOR MIND POLLUTION

Real people meet real people. Fakes meet fakes. Your relationships are transformed with an open mind and heart. The person you choose as a partner is a reflection of *you.*

The good news is that the moment you decide that what you know is more important than what you have been taught to believe, you have shifted gears in your quest for abundance. Success comes from within not from without. (*Emerson*)

Countless clients have overcome limitations of their false selves. They have learned it is possible to go from "woe is me!" to "wow, I'm free!"

AWARENESS PRACTICE

Awareness practice is a powerful technique to keep you out of the fault pollution. Think of your brain as a series of railway tracks with thousands of stations. The brain can be trained to travel to magnificent destinations. Train it to lay tracks to places that enhance love and life.

Declaring your intentions is one way to start laying those tracks. By declaring what you intend to do and repeating the words as a mantra, you become more centered and focused. Don't be discouraged; your brain will make the new connections, and you will expand your thinking.

Most people give up on goals too soon. Dr. Wayne Drevets, a renowned neuroscientist said, "In the brain, practice makes permanent."

When Janet first began repeating to herself, "I like and appreciate myself just the way I am," it was followed by her thought, "What a joke!" It has taken years to program your brain, which likes the familiar routes it has taken before.

When you are laying your new tracks, your brain may be drawn back to its destructive directions like the old embers of self-doubt. However, continued practice and repeating your goals will win out, and your new destinations will be reached.

Your brain has more than one million billion neuron connections, so you have a lot of power! Get ready to reroute connections and sustain change; just don't give up before the new railroad is complete.

Once your new railroad is complete, you can deal with any threat of derailment, as Janet found out. When her date attempted to put her down with a cutting remark, she told herself, "I like myself the way I am," then calmly let him know put-downs were off limits. Through months of practice, she had trained herself to respond assertively even when she was threatened by someone attempting to diminish her.

> No one can make you feel inferior without your consent. (Eleanor Roosevelt)

Your Turn

This following exercise can be done alone or as a couple. If you do this practice together, you can improve together and understand what an impact you have on each other.

Think of a sentence you can use to enhance feelings of self-worth. Write it, say it, or even sing it as often as possible to retrain your brain.

Practice your sentence numerous times a day for a month or more and see if it makes a difference. If it works, continue to practice until you think that you have made some progress. You can also share statements of intention with a close friend or your partner and set times to compare progress. Keep reporting your intention to send your brain train in the direction of positive, healthy intentions in keeping with your values and purpose.

> You can virtually influence your life from within by auto affirmation. The first thing each morning, and the last thing each night, suggest to yourself specific ideas that you wish to embody in your character and personality. Address such suggestions to yourself, silently or aloud, until they are deeply impressed upon your mind. (Grenville Kleiser)

Although it seemed magical when the direction of Janet's thinking changed tracks, what seemed like a magical moment was the result of ꞏting her positive intention for months.

Do not give up too soon. It takes time and practice for statements of intention to work. "Patience and perseverance have a magical effect" (John Quincy Adams).

You can do individual intentions or intentions as a couple. An example for a couple might be, "We now have our ideal relationship." Friendship on fire is an ideal; derailments happen, but statements of intention help you get back on track.

Keep Love Glowing

Josie's parents were married for half a century and still maintained a *friendship on fire* after six children and many life hurdles. As Josie's mother was dying, her father sat beside the bed and took his wife's hand. "Baby, it's OK to go. I will find you again." Following his words, she literally took her last breath. Josie was touched beyond words to see this affection between her parents.

STABLE ANCHOR

It is important to honor our need for connection and lasting relationships. A lasting and loving relationship provides a stable anchor in a demanding world.

> Let us love one another in this brief time for we shall die in exile
> far from home. (May Sarton)

THE RAIN OF KINDNESS

Researcher René Spitz was quite concerned when she realized babies in orphanages died at alarming rates even though they were fed and clothed. We now call this failure-to-thrive syndrome. Babies are wired to need food, clothing, shelter, and a loving connection. This connection with the human touch and caring from someone in a loving way enhances life from infancy, and the need for it continues throughout life regardless of age. The human touch can calm us and make us feel loved, wanted, and part of something more than ourselves.

We weep when light does not reach our hearts.
We wither like fields if someone close does not rain their kindness upon us. (Meister Eckhart)

Mother Teresa said, "The biggest disease today is not leprosy or tuberculosis but rather the feeling of not belonging." *Friendship on fire* is part of the solution. Do not be hard on yourself as you remove your barriers to closeness. Your brain is always trying to protect you. If you think of what has happened in the past as lessons instead of failures, you will be on the path to growth. We do make progress until we can accept where we are.

MEAN VS. MEANINGFUL

It is so tempting to allow the petty frustrations of daily life with children to turn you into a shamer and blamer. You can become a mean machine focused on how the dishes should be stacked in the cabinet or the way your partner shuts the door.

Josie recalls that her mother told her she could choose mean or meaningful ways to relate. If she chose mean, she would suffer; but if she approached each day in search of meaning and celebration, she could live in the love. Josie's parents resolved incidents of criticism and contempt, honored and respected one another, and maintained love until the end.

HOW MUCH LOVE

I nearly died when I was fifty-two. As I faded in and out of consciousness, I had a profound awareness that the only thing that mattered about my life was how much I had loved. Learning to love and accept ourselves and others is a journey.

Friendship on fire is a powerful connection. Partners respect the power they have over one another. They support one another through the growing pains of becoming unstuck and living in the moment. As you become more capable of repair and compassion and less likely to resort to ego eruptions, you are moving in the right direction.

Your Turn

Reminder: All the "Your Turn" sections can be done alone or as a couple.

Focus on your breath. Take seven deep breaths and count each in your mind. Notice where you feel tension in your body. Imagine that the tension is a knot that you can untie. Just let it go. If other thoughts enter your mind, that is OK. Just refocus on your breath; breathe deeply, down to your diaphragm.

Picture a beautiful, peaceful scene and go there in your mind. Maybe it is the beach, maybe the mountains; go there in your mind, see what you see, hear what you hear, and touch what you touch. Allow yourself to become more relaxed. Now repeat the following phrases in your mind:

- May I like and accept myself just as I am.
- May I be filled with loving kindness.
- May I give and receive loving kindness.
- May I experience true joy alone and with others.
- May I be at peace.

Imagine that you are enveloped in a golden, healing light from God. Feel and picture yourself absorbing the light through your skin and allow this golden light to be carried into your veins and arteries to comfort and heal you. Breathe deeply and slowly as the warmth moves through your body. Take your time.

Notice or imagine your partner is in the room with you. Take a moment to picture sending healing light through your heart out to your partner. You are healing your heart with the light from God and sending it out to your partner.

With the in breath, imagine that your body is spacious enough to hold negative emotions. Acknowledge and accept these negative emotions. With the out breath, imagine that you breathe out healing to yourself and others.

If you do not currently have a partner, send the light toward someone in your family. Use this visualization when you need to heal your heart or repair hurts.

Choose "meaningful" instead of "mean".

Rebuilding the Fire

Monica, a spunky thirty-three-year-old, announced during her first therapy session that she had flunked relationships. "No more men in my life!" In her mind, her love life was kaput after being dumped by yet another guy.

SIDELINED

I asked, "If you plan to be sidelined for life, why are you sitting here with a relationship therapist?"

When Monica retorted, "I need support after being dumped again!" I then clarified that the therapy sessions were to help her learn from failure. They would focus on what it takes to succeed in a relationship, and then she could choose if she wanted back in the game.

DISTANCE FROM OLD PATTERNS

Gradually, Monica was able to understand her attraction to bait-and-switch types—guys that did a huge sales job in the beginning then faded away. Her father had a similar pattern with her long-suffering mother. Rather than be like her mother, Monica had decided to cut her losses at thirty-three.

Monica worked hard in therapy to figure out why she flunked relationships. She eventually decided to get off the bench and look for guys who have what it takes to go the distance.

NICE GUYS FINISH FIRST

It was evident Monica was making progress when she described running into her most recent failure in the grocery store with his new girlfriend. She had turned to a young stranger dressed in a professional pantsuit who was standing next to her in the produce department and said, "See that guy and woman over there? That is my ex and his new girlfriend. He likes to change every few years. Take my advice and avoid those bait-and-switch types."

The young stranger laughed out loud and then agreed wholeheartedly. By reaching out to another person in the grocery, Monica was beginning to distance herself from her old pattern. Humor helped her to distance herself from her hopelessness and feelings of alienation.

After several years, I received an upbeat card from Monica with the message, "Nice guys finish first!" She was happily married and expecting a baby.

AVOID GAMERS AND BLAMERS

Relationships are teachers. If you are considering a commitment to someone, be sure that when they describe past relationships, they tell you mistakes they made and avoid blaming the other person for everything that went wrong.

Those who are capable of friendship on fire take responsibility for their choices and past patterns of behavior. Avoid deflecting blamers and manipulative gamers.

Have you learned more from success or failure? Most learn more from their failures. Each relationship failure teaches you something about yourself and others. Each encounter teaches us more about ourselves.

LOVE LESSONS

Love is tough and demands the best from you. *If you listen* to the lessons, you will get better and become more mature. A friendship on fire is a work in progress and evolves and grows toward increased love and safety. Mistakes in relationships are best viewed as a nudge or a shove in the direction of love for self and others.

"LIVE YOUR WAY TO THE ANSWERS"

As you look back on failed relationships, you may realize that those learning experiences helped prepare you for the ability to maintain a long-term intimate relationship. Look at yourself; learn your lessons; and, as Rainer Maria Rilke once said, "live your way to the answers".

Your Turn

Think back on relationship tests that you flunked and reflect on what you learned. Then consider where you learned this behavior. You may want to share these observations with your partner or a close friend.

For example,

- Behavior: I became hysterical when under stress.
- History: This was my mom's all-purpose solution to problems.
- Learning: This did not work well for Mom who had a heart attack at fifty-four, and it has not worked for me.

Instead, you should think, "I will practice handling my feelings in a calm and firm way through statements of intention, visualization, and awareness exercises."

AWARENESS EXERCISE

Find a comfortable place to sit or lie down, close your eyes, and focus on your breathing. Allow your hand to rest gently on your stomach and feel the rising and falling as you breathe. Take seven deep breaths, counting each one in your mind. If other thoughts enter your mind, that is OK. Just notice the thought and refocus on the breath.

Notice where there is strong discomfort or tension in your body. What happens when you allow your attention to focus on that sensation? How does it change? Scan through your body for tightness and allow muscles to release a bit. You do not need all that tension.

Just as your gentle awareness can create shifts in your body, the same process can unfold as you turn kind awareness on your thoughts. Your thoughts are just passing through your mind. You are not your thoughts; they are not the truth of things. You are much more than your thoughts.

Imagine that as each thought arises, you can encase it in a bubble and send it to God for healing, letting go of thoughts as they pass through you mind, letting go of tension.

As you allow thoughts to float away, ask God to return thoughts that are good for you in a loving and healing way. God is love. Let go of toxic judgments of self and others based on past conditioning, and trust God to send you the thoughts that will help you live in love and wisdom—letting go of old tapes and toxic thoughts in your head, opening yourself to receive higher wisdom, expanding your capacity for loving kindness toward yourself and others, embracing feelings of peace and serenity.

When your mind wanders away from the focus on peace and healing, simply notice your thoughts and return to the breathing without criticism or condemnation. Just return to the sensations of breathing.

Focus your attention on the present moment. Now is all there is. The future and the past do not exist in this moment. Release destructive thought habits and practice embracing the here and now. Let yourself unfold in the present moment.

As you practice, your ability to remain present in the here and now will expand—no holding, no tension—allowing painful thoughts and sensations to float in an accepting openness.

Open your eyes when you are ready. It is best to practice this several times a day for a few minutes. Release your despair into the boundless presence of God.

Past Ignites Present

It is important to understand not intellectually, but actually in your daily life how you have built up images about your wife, your child, your country, your leaders . . . These images create a space between you and what you observe and in that space there is conflict.
— Jiddu Krishnamurti

Leah was an intelligent, outgoing student who was swept away by her handsome literature professor. He seemed amazingly and attractively older and wiser. When he hit on her after class one day, she was dazzled right into the sack.

The prof asked Leah to marry him, but all her instincts shouted no! She told him she needed time to sort things out. When the prof became obsessed with Leah and began to stalk her, she scheduled a therapy appointment to help her gain perspective on how to handle the situation with integrity.

WHAT IS REAL?

She was heartsick about the prof; her college life was in turmoil. Together, we worked on determining why Leah's brain had taken a long lunch break and missed the warning signs.

We solved the puzzle by piecing together Leah's life before she met the prof. It is not necessary to dwell on the past, but it helps to understand what past decisions you made about life affect how you see the world. Once you realize why you see people the way you do, you are free to make different choices. It helps to ask yourself, "What is real in this situation?"

Since you see what you *expect* to see, you can understand your behavior through the lens of your past. Leah saw the prof through expectations she had formed in childhood. As a baby, Leah was abandoned by her mother and adopted by her loving uncle and aunt, who were teachers. They saved her from hardship as an orphan.

FLASH MAGNETISM

In her naiveté, Leah generalized that handsome male teachers were kind and safe. The prof was appealing partly because he reminded her, unconsciously, of her handsome uncle Ben. Her brain also generalized that older guys like her uncle Ben were big teddy bears. Leah's lens of the past limited her perspective.

Think of your brain like a magnet that is attracted and fascinated by the familiar. We project the good the bad and the ugly of our past onto the screen of the present. Our brain loves the familiar.

RERUNS

Practices of awareness and mindfulness help you recognize rerun movies in your brain so you can remind yourself to focus on what is real in the present moment.

On the surface, these two men seemed the same, but they were very different. She projected Uncle Ben's character onto the prof and could not see the real volatile person. She believed that any minute, this man-child would morph into a kind and loving father figure. When she faced reality, she realized most of her blue funk was a result of her familiar reruns.

YOU GET WHAT YOU EXPECT

It's amazing how the brain sees familiar images instead of reality; you get what you expect. Your mind clings to what you know. Patterns that protected you in the past can turn into burdens.

Once Leah understood more about the map of her mind, she was able to comprehend her attraction, see the prof realistically with compassion, and move on. Leah's brain fooled her into thinking history was repeating itself when it was not; it just appeared that way to her brain. Why? Her brain was searching for familiar images.

THE PAST ONLY APPEARS TO REPEAT ITSELF

The prof seemed to offer a safe relationship like the one she had enjoyed with Uncle Ben, and he was able to lead her into the fascinating world of literature. As she got to know him better, she realized that she wouldn't be safe with him, nor was it likely that he would be able to maintain her interest and respect. Unlike her Uncle Ben, he was unstable; and while he could talk to her about life, books, art, and the places he had traveled, he always had to be a lecturer in charge of the discussion. Unlike Uncle Ben, he was basically insecure, hence his need to be validated by the adulation of younger women.

THE BRAIN LOVES FAME

Your brain loves familiar patterns because they feel safe, but that doesn't make them so. You need to get curious and check it out when your senses are telling you something isn't right. Neuroscientists have an expression that "the brain loves fame." Thoughts that are popular in your mind affect who and what attracts you. In order to develop a friendship on fire, you need to

- ➤ observe your programmed movies on a screen in your mind,
- ➤ become conscious of what you want to create in the present,
- ➤ let go of fear, and
- ➤ create a new reality tale.

CONNECT THE DOTS

The beginning of a relationship is like a connect-the-dots picture with very few dots connected; you don't get the real and complete picture. In the beginning, most of what you see is pictures from your own past. Over time, you get to know the person, connect more dots, and begin to see the real person.

You need to love the questions and hold them close to your heart but you must live your way to the answers. (Rainer Maria Rilke)

Your Turn

Imagine a phrase that summarizes each important person in your life.

For example, Leah might describe Uncle Ben as "a loving husband and father, wise and beloved teacher." She might say the professor is "brilliant and mercurial, dedicated his life to literature."

Write a sentence that summarizes each important person in your life and their values. Then ask yourself these questions:

- Do you see connections between important people in your past and patterns in your current relationship?
- What part do you play in destructive patterns?
- Can you commit to changing your role in negative patterns?
- What positive patterns have you replicated in you relationship?
- How can you appreciate and build on the positive patterns?

MINDFULNESS PRACTICE FOR DEPRESSED FEELINGS

Close your eyes and focus on your breathing. Allow your hand to rest gently on your stomach and feel the rising and falling as you breathe. Take seven deep breathes counting each one in your mind. If other thoughts enter your mind, that is OK just notice the thought and refocus on the breath.

Notice where there is strong discomfort or tension in your body. What happens when you allow your attention to focus on that sensation? How does it change? Scan through your body for tightness and allow muscles to release a bit. You do not need all that tension.

Just as your gentle awareness can create shifts in your body, the same process can unfold as you turn kind awareness on your thoughts. Your thoughts are just passing through your mind. You are not your thoughts; they are not the truth of things. You are much more than your thoughts.

Imagine that as each thought arises that you can encase it in a bubble and send it to God for healing. Letting go of thoughts as they pass through your mind . . . Letting go of tension.

As you allow thoughts to float away ask God to return thoughts that are good for you in a loving and healing way. God is love . . . . Let go of toxic judgments of self and others based on past conditioning and trust God to send you the thoughts that will help you live in love and wisdom . . . Letting go of old tapes in your head, opening yourself to receive Higher Wisdom . . . Letting go of toxic thoughts . . . Expanding your capacity for loving kindness toward yourself and others; embracing feelings of peace and serenity.

When your mind wanders away from the focus on peace and healing, simply notice your thoughts and return to the breath without criticism or condemnation. Just return to the sensations of the breath.

Focus your attention on the present moment. Now is all there is. The future and the past do not exist in this moment.

Release destructive thought habits and practice embracing the here and now. Let yourself unfold in the present moment. As you practice your ability to remain present in the here and now will expand. No holding, no tension . . . allowing painful thoughts and sensations to float in an accepting openness.

Open your eyes when you are ready. It is best to practice this several times a day for a few minutes. Release your despair into the boundless presence of God.

Patterns of Fire

John met Mary Ann at Happy Hour and was pleased to learn that she worked in his building. They quickly became an item, and friends referred to the attractive young pair as Ken and Barbie.

When Mary Ann lost her job, John told her she could stay in his apartment until she started her new job the next month. Almost immediately after moving in, Mary Ann became moody and unpredictable. John felt like he was on a roller coaster.

SACK FACTS

As I explained to John when he came for therapy, you get to know a person's style of relating as you see them in many different circumstances over time like a connect-the-dots picture.

John made the sack mistake. He was in the sack with Mary Ann before he took time to connect the dots. Most of the information that John had about this new woman in his life were sack facts, and those looked phenomenal! Sack facts gave John no clue about the whole picture.

Unfortunately, Mary Ann had a disorganized attachment style, and the relationship ended in a few months.

Your Turn

Research has identified four common attachment styles and their characteristics. Which pattern best fits you? Which attachment style are you attracted to?

1. *Healthy:* Are you and your partner able to be both close and apart?
2. *Ambivalent:* Sometimes connects and then abruptly distances from partner out of fear or anger? Do you and our partner do this kind of dance?
3. *Avoidant:* Avoids relationships out of fear? Are you afraid of closeness?
4. *Disorganized:* Frequently overreacts and acts out at the drop of a hat? Often feels confused about thoughts and feelings in a relationship? Do you and your partner feel like you are on a roller coaster?

Answer the questions as a starting point for a healthy attachment style needed for *friendship on fire.*

When working with your partner on questions, the answers should not be used as ammunition against one another. Remember, your goal is a better relationship. Everyone has faults, and the goal is to not cut the other person down; so together, you can alter your style of relating.

> You must be the change you wish to see in the world. (Mahatma Gandhi)

Addiction Snuffs Fire

Dave was a thirty-nine-year-old who became addicted to Internet pornography. Over the years, Alice, his wife of eighteen years, gave him many warnings about his addiction; however, he was unable to control this impulse. When she told him he had to either quit it entirely or leave, Dave was devastated. Her ultimatum was a wake-up call. He was about to lose his wife and three children, the four loves of his life.

UNQUIET MIND

When Dave came for therapy, it became clear he used his porn viewing and chat rooms as an escape from deep inner suffering. When his mind was quiet, he was ruthless in self-condemnation and insecurity. He lacked a feeling of inner value.

As the oldest son in a family of high achievers, he recalled that when his father died when he was four years old, relatives said, "You are the man of the house now."

FEARFUL MEMORIES

He did his best to be a "little man" and act brave with his two younger sisters. He took his perceived responsibility very seriously. Inside he was fearful; he felt overwhelmed and was afraid of not living up to the expectation of being the man of the house. As an adult, he would lose himself in a fantasy world as a means of avoiding the reruns of old movies of inadequacy. Instead of opening the door to his fears and learning to sit with his thoughts, he escaped into cyberspace. This was a reason, not an excuse. For example, Dave might honestly say he used addictions to escape his hateful memories, but he still needed to face himself. Like so many people I have seen, Dave needed to pick up his fear and stare it in the face.

MINDFUL AWARENESS

> When unattended, our thinking runs our lives without us even knowing it. Attended with mindful awareness, we have a chance not only to know ourselves better and see what is on our minds but also to hold our thoughts differently with greater wisdom, so they no longer rule our lives. (Jon Kabat-Zinn)

Addictions are powerful and may be relationship wreckers. To change this level of power, it is important to begin with a practice of self-acceptance. This is why Alcoholics Anonymous testimonials begin with the admission, "I am an alcoholic." Self-hatred underlies many issues in a relationship, literally from A to Z, from addictions to zealotism.

MASKS

A lack of deep inner value prevents true intimacy since you do not want others to see you as you are. Living behind a mask takes a toll on you and your relationships. Taking off your mask and allowing others to see your authentic self is challenging. The road to recovery requires time, commitment, and practice.

EGO SPEAK

The poet Rainer Maria Rilke wrote, "Let me surrender to the powers greater than myself."

This is what is required to deal with an addiction; you are so caught up in your own ego that it interferes with love for others and self. Dave admitted to himself and his wife for the first time that he had a problem, found a twelve-step program for his addiction, and got on the road to recovery.

LET GO AND LET GOD

The twelve steps helped Dave move out of his ego and listen to his higher self. In therapy, we practiced noticing his ego thoughts and putting them on a small sheet of paper in his mind. Then we would fill the balloon with helium and imagine letting it float up to God to help him find solutions. He did this almost constantly at first and would scribble thoughts like, "I will never measure up" or "I am worthless" and send them off in balloons. Like many people I have worked with, Dave reported that it felt like a miracle when he was led to people, experiences, and books that were exactly what he needed.

In my work over three decades, I have watched many such everyday miracles of transformation as people let go of the toxic ego tapes and surrender to a higher power.

"We're entirely ready to have God remove all these defects of character" (step 6, Alcoholics Anonymous).

Your Turn

If you struggle with an addiction, consider whether this blocks the kind of relationship that you want. Research what type of help you are willing to accept.

TWELVE STEPS

You may decide to get help through spiritual guidance or decide on a self-help group. Membership in twelve-step groups is informal. The only requirement is a desire to stop the addiction. A key principle for a twelve-step group is anonymity for members. There are no membership costs. Meetings range from small groups of two or three to groups of five hundred or more in large metropolitan areas. The style of meetings ranges from speaker meetings, where one or two people share their stories from a podium, to discussion and step studies, which invite participation from those present.

Meeting schedules and directions to meetings can be found on the Web in many communities, and twelve-step groups are also listed in the white pages of most telephone directories, usually by the name of the addiction they address. If you are in a relationship with someone with addiction problems, there are also Al-Anon and codependency groups listed.

Friendship Fuels Respect

People seldom improve when they have no model but themselves to copy.
—Oliver Goldsmith

If you want friendship on fire, imitate the Brady Bunch (I'm not referring to the TV *Brady Bunch)*. I'm talking about James Brady, press secretary to former president Ronald Reagan. Brady was shot during the assassination attempt on the president on March 30, 1981.

REALITY TALES

When Brady and his wife, Sarah, appear together, it is inspiring to see how they pulled together after a tragedy. Brady may have difficulty with his speech, but he also has great perspective on life and a remarkable sense of humor and humility. He remarked, "The doctors saved me physically, but my wife saved me emotionally." The spark and spirit of their friendship-on-fire glow on the screen.

Why do we look to movies and TV for relationship models instead of real-life success stories? We know that the chance of these Hollywood-style relationships lasting is about the same as winning lotto! They are our modern-day fairy tales, a rewrite of the Snow-White-Cinderella syndrome. What we need are reality tales.

What about true stories of people like the Bradys who maintain close bonds despite great odds? There are many such models. As I write this I have just learned about the death of Paul Newman. I am reminded about all that he and Joanne Woodward accomplished as a couple in their long marriage through charitable donations from the sale of food products.Both these couples are role models for lasting and loving unions.

The brain tends to act upon the pictures in our mind's eye: what you see is what you get. Think about who you see as your relationship role models. Are they a Hollywood façade or the real deal? Those with *friendship on fire* help one another share their talent with others. Love is a verb and is sustained by action.

Friendship on fire inspires us to give. *Friendship on fire* is not lust or a passing fancy; it is devotion to the good of our partner and a better world. A *friendship on fire* burns on the fuel of mutual kindness and respect.

> One of the miracles of lasting love is the power of seeing through its own enchantments and yet not being disenchanted. (C. S. Lewis)

WRITING A REALITY TALE

Your Turn

What are some of the behaviors that you have seen in exceptional models of lasting and loving relationships? What can you do to practice those in your relationship?

Brady examples:

- devotion
- caretaking
- mutual respect
- humor
- shared values
- partnership
- admiration
- standing up for what they believe

Which of the qualities that you most respect do you have? Which ones do you share in your relationship? What values do you want to express as a couple? Think of a couple who lives these values. What do you need to work on to be more like them? Respect yourself and one another. Express your deepest values in your relationship.

Control Can Singe

When Tony came to see me, he was facing a second divorce. Tony was a fortysomething successful swashbuckling entrepreneur. I had to work hard to get a word in during the first session with this fast-talking, take-charge guy.

TAKE-CHARGE TENDENCY

As it turned out, his take-charge tendency had led to relationship problems. He grew up in a very outgoing and emotional Italian family. Although they talked over one another and played verbal fastball, there was a lot of love and loyalty.

The youngest child in the family was his developmentally disabled sister, Maggie. As the eldest son, Tony spent quite a bit of time as protector and caretaker.

BACK TO THE FAMILIAR

As an adult, Tony was drawn to women who unconsciously reminded him of Maggie. He was hooked on rerun thinking. Both of his long-term relationships had been with immature and unstable women. He reverted to the familiar: his older and wiser role. Eventually, this wore thin with both wives, and they served him divorce papers instead of dinner.

Because Tony was such an alpha male, he wanted all the control; his partners did not have the emotional strength to stand up to him. Both labeled him as controlling before they cut and ran.

He was crushed because, in his heart, he knew he was a good guy who had given a lot in both relationships.

I pointed out, "You take the floor most of the time. Could this be one of the reasons you have had problems with your relationships?"

THE LIST

Tony made a list of many characteristics he wanted so he could make a conscious choice: strong, confident, stable, loyal, and dominant without being domineering. By itemizing all of the qualities he sought in a woman, he was recognizing his own past failures and the personality type that would keep his overbearing nature in check.

THE LIST RISK

Years later, I ran into Tony at a store. He was ecstatic! He was engaged to someone who could handle his alpha wolf. He laughed as he explained that he had kept his list in his wallet when he began dating again. When he met Ms. Alpha for a date, she asked him to sit down for a talk before they went out!

He told her that he had learned when to keep his mouth shut. She produced a list of things she was looking for in a man and informed him that she did not want to waste time going out unless he was in the ballpark. He was! He then produced *his* list.

The "list risk" remains a joke between them. They now have a *friendship on fire*.

Your Turn

If you have no significant other at the moment, think of characteristics that you want in a partner. Make two columns: in the first column, write down a list of desired characteristics. In the second, write characteristics of bad choices in past relationships. Figure out why certain patterns may have been familiar and attractive. The familiar may be attracting you to the wrong kind of person, so work harder; give this some serious thought.

Review the characteristics and the reasons they are on the list until you are satisfied that this is what you really desire. Use this list to keep you on track. What do you really hope to find in another person? Don't be distracted by Hollywood-borne notions of what should be right for you. Think about what warms you toward another. What kind of person does it take to light your fire?

These are some of the things that Tony wanted:

- Strong. Why? So she can handle my boisterous nature.
- Confident. Why? To stop me when I am out of line.

Past bad choices:

- Needy. Good in a sister, bad choice in a mate.
- Overprotective. My handicapped sister needed me so she would feel calm and safe.

Firebreaks Can Be Mistakes

Liana, a high-powered executive, was quite a package—successful, intelligent, and attractive; yet, when it came to relationships, she was clueless. She had been programmed by her alcoholic family. She shut down as soon as she walked through the door of her childhood home since she never knew when things would explode.

SCANNING FOR DANGER

As an adult, when she walked into a room, she habitually scanned for danger and remained quiet and withdrawn as she read the emotional climate. Instead of being proactive, she was reactive in her relationships. She let men choose her. She did not feel safe enough to reach out for intimacy. As a child, Liana learned to protect herself, to act as if everything was just peachy.

YOU ATTRACT WHAT YOU THINK ABOUT

She developed a great act. She appeared confident and in control. Many inaccurately read her behavior as stuck-up. Her beautiful and confident act was so good that her married boss fell for her. Liana's unconscious self-protection told her it was safer to be involved with a married boss than someone who was available. Why? Because if she lived with someone, things would get out of control. Since her parents had such a caustic relationship fueled by alcohol and drugs, she believed that fleeting moments of happiness had to be stolen.

Since Liana's mind movies were all about danger, that is what she attracted. Through her lack of awareness, she put herself in a situation where her job was on the line.

POWER KEGS

Her solution led her straight toward a power keg. Although it may seem strange that Liana saw an affair with her boss as less risky than *friendship on fire*, when you understand her history, it makes sense. She had no knowledge of how amazing lasting relationships can be and kept people at a distance for self-protection. Liana decided, "Relationships are too dangerous full-time. Moments of happiness are fleeting and must be stolen." She chose a married man because she believed that if she kept her distance, she would have more control.

When someone decides to have an affair, his or her reasoning might be, "I'm afraid of getting too close to someone, so I need to slink out and sneak some moments of love." Many believe that keeping their distance protects them. Affairs create distance between all the parties involved.

Your Turn

Look at some of your past relationship blunders. Was the blunder based on behavior that once protected you? What kinds of things do you do for self-protection based on past learning? Maintain distance? Act too clingy? Do some of both?

Remember what it was like in your family as a child, and write down what first comes to mind. What decisions did you make about self-protection? Was your childhood homelife experience

- loving?
- joyful?
- negative?
- destructive?
- boring?
- explosive?
- unpredictable?
- depressing?
- confusing?

- chaotic?
- rigid?

Write a sentence that expresses your decision: "Family life was dull and boring. I will only find happiness outside my home," or "My family is so chaotic that I need to always be in control."

Do you recall making stupid decisions in your relationships? Write down what the circumstances were and how these decisions were intended to protect you.

See if you can trace your actions back to childhood lessons. You do not need to be imprisoned by a past that depletes your energy. You can fire up your life by making new decisions. When you are making a bad decision about relationships, there is a logical reason from the past. It does not help to judge yourself or have friends ask, "How can you be with such a jerk?" Ask yourself, how did this behavior protect me in the past?

1. Why is the pattern so familiar?
2. Do I feel I need to grab happiness for a moment because it cannot last?
3. How did it serve me in my family to be distant? a pleaser? a clown? a rebel? some other role?
4. Am I stuck in certain roles in a relationship? How do I want to be in a relationship?
5. How do my past "mistakes" in relationships make sense based on what I learned from family? community? books? media? peers?

Write a paragraph that describes your perfect friendship on fire and refer to it from time to time.

Flash in the Pan Disappoints

Beverly, twenty-two, grew up comparing herself to images of perfect skinny models in fashion magazines. She wanted her hair, nails, figure, face, clothes, and shoes to look as good as those on the cover of *Vogue*. She believed that she needed to look perfect to be seen as a foxy lady of her town.

FALSE FRONTS

What was the real Beverly like? She wasn't sure. She spent so much time and effort being a faux foxy lady that there was no time left to discover herself. She was afraid to wake up without makeup—to be the real deal: no pretenses, no masks, no false fronts.

PRINCE CHARMING: TROLL IN DISGUISE?

As I noted earlier, real people meet real people. Fakes meet fakes. Prince Charming may turn out to be a troll in disguise. The fairy princess may be a witch. Appearances are deceiving, and so are the fronts people project to manipulate each other. An authentic relationship, one that can endure for a lifetime, is grounded in acceptance based on mutual understanding. To be authentic is to be genuine, willing to share your true self with another and willing to accept the responsibility of defining yourself, unclouded by your fears of how you are perceived. You have a life purpose, and it is up to you to discover and live your mission.

"WHO ARE YOU, AND WHAT DO YOU WANT?"

A philosopher once recorded this message on his answering machine: "Who are you, and what do you want?"

These are two of the most important questions you can ask yourself and your partner. Only the two of you can answer them for yourselves.

Your Turn

Get out a notebook or journal, and answer the following questions:

- How can you increase the love in your life and decrease false pride and ego?
- Do you present a false self to the world?
- Do you present a false self in your relationship?
- How did it protect you in the past to develop a false self?
- Do you recall when you first developed a false self?
- Does your false self protect you now?
- How can you begin to be more authentic in your life?
- How can you be more authentic in your relationship?
- How can you do a better job of nurturing yourself?
- Do you tend to be too passive or too aggressive in your relationship?
- How can you get a better balance?

The following will help you identify your true values. Imagine it is your funeral, and answer the following:

- What do you want people to say about your life?
- What do you want to stand for?
- What is your purpose?
- How would your ideal obituary read?

In Beverly's case, what she wrote was quite different from how she was living. Her obituary read,

Beverly loved animals and devoted much of her time to rescuing greyhound dogs. She was spontaneous, fun-loving, and had spent a lot of time in nature studying animal behavior. She was a beloved wife and mother known for speaking her mind.

If you are in a relationship, consider how secure you and your partner are to be real with yourselves and with one another. Write down what areas you consider real. List three ways that you can increase your safety to be authentic and real with one another.

Discuss how you can adopt these new behaviors with one another, and focus on achieving your true happiness and fulfillment. Sing your own song. Those with friendship on fire know the song in one another's hearts and can sing it back when their partner cannot recall the words.

You Hold the Matches

We lose the fear of making decisions, great and small, as we realize that should our choice prove wrong we can, if we will, learn from experience.

—Bill W.

Anna is a thirty-four-year-old nurse who is magnetically attracted to the traveling salesman type. These are the guys who give a great sales pitch then travel. They are warm and fuzzy for a while and make an escape like a jackrabbit. In therapy, Anna decided to use 20/20 hindsight to make better future choices. She vowed to research her new boyfriend's background at the start of a new relationship. If he had a traveling salesman history, she would cross him off her list.

THE TSM TYPE

Anna developed a list of desirable attributes in her ideal man. She thought she might not find one that would make the 100 percent category, but he had to come in at least at 80 percent. In the checkout period, if the traveling salesman mode (TSM) showed up, he was an automatic out. There would no longer be the three or more strikes and you're out routine. The TSM topped her "I don't go for that" list.

FACING THE FORCE

One night at a party, Anna made a breakthrough when a TSM hit on her. Since her magnetic response was activated by his aftershave, she decided to do some quick research. She discovered that this rakish rambler had a date across the room that was bringing him a drink while he hit on her. He was out.

I DON'T GO FOR THAT

"I don't go for that" is an important concept. Successful relationships are based on kindness and consideration and not simply on charm. When behaviors are troublesome to either partner, the "I don't go for that" principle kicks in. Over time, *friendship on fire* candidates memorize the behaviors they refuse to accept. They do not need to yell, scream, or make a scene because they don't allow themselves to become victims. Anna maintained her poise and integrity as she excused herself from the TSM and moved on to better pastures.

When Anna finally met her ideal guy, she told him calmly and firmly that he was a wonderful person; but if he did not want a committed relationship, she did not want to stay involved. He showed her with his behavior and words that he meant to stick around.

Your Turn

Do you recognize self-destructive patterns in your choice of partners? The brain loves the familiar because it keeps us safe. At times, people hold on for dear life rather than make a change. This is often clear in abuse situations. When an abused child is being removed from the offenders, he hangs on to what he knows.

Are you holding on to the familiar in a destructive situation? Have you picked the wrong partners based on what is familiar?

List two behaviors that you do not go for in a partner. Those with a *friendship on fire* make their boundaries and expectations clear up front; they honor the standards of the other. Stand up for yourself. Over time, if someone does not heed your boundaries, vote with your feet.

Disappointment is a powerful teacher. It shows us the ways we are stuck in our limited egos and helps us open up to a deeper experience in life and love. Begin to consider the following questions:

- Am I able to use disappointments to help me open my life to spirit and love?
- Does disappointment make me bitter or better?
- How can I learn to live more in the present moment, learn my lessons from disappointments, and move on?
- How do I keep myself stuck in self-destructive patterns and how can I choose a path toward enlightenment and fulfillment?

"Love is nature's second sun" (proverb from Holland).

Fire Power

Juanita, a thirty-year-old Hispanic social worker, was savvy about relationships because she specialized in marriage and family therapy. Her first marriage ended in divorce, so she was determined to make her second marriage work. After her divorce, she went to therapy and realized her first husband was a clone of her distant father. She quipped that if she had searched, she could not have found a better reproduction.

STEPS AWAY FROM THE DREAM

Because of her relationship knowledge and work and having grown older and wiser about her relationship needs, she had developed a clear picture of what she wanted. She wrote it down, but she wasn't prepared for her next adventure. Her dream was only steps away but she could not see it yet.

For several years, she repeatedly told herself, "I thank God for my ideal relationship" and pictured a wedding by a lake in detail. It is a powerful practice to express faith and gratitude in your statements of intention.

It turned out that her ideal relationship was with Jose, who had attended her church for years. One Wednesday, it dawned on her that she'd been sitting in church with her perfect relationship partner every Sunday for five years!

DREAMS ARE IN YOUR NEIGHBORHOOD

When Juanita retrained her brain to look for what she wanted, she realized he was already in her neighborhood. We see what we expect to see. For example, Inuit families in extremely cold climates see over one hundred kinds of snow because their brain has been trained to recognize the difference. Train your brain to think of possibilities. Positive thoughts and intentions help you create a reality tale of love and healing. Picture your life as you want it to be, not as things were before.

CLEAR INTENTION

As you focus your mind with clear intention, your unconscious moves in the direction of your goal. Have you ever had the experience of wanting a certain kind of car and then seeing them everywhere? This is because your conscious mind can only focus on seven things while your unconscious has unlimited capacity. Right now, your unconscious is operating your entire body; so if you turn your attention to how you are sitting, you will realize that you unconsciously moved your muscles and positioned yourself. Statements of intention help you program your brain in the direction of your dreams.

BRAIN SPOTLIGHTS

As I write this, we are looking forward to the birth of a new grandson in a month. I see pregnant women, babies, and little boys everywhere I go these days. The spotlight in my brain shines on diapers and baby products in the grocery since my unconscious is primed to notice such things; last year, I could have tripped over baby stuff and not noticed. Although I have ignored the baby isle for years, my spotlight is focused on bambino items because this happening is important to me. Self-program your brain with what is most important to you.

In your heart, you know the secrets to your happiness. Let your statements and intention remind you of who you truly are.

SHARED DREAMS

Not only did Jose share Juanita's values on work, family, and spirituality, but they also shared a sense of wonder about the world and interest in science.

Your brain follows the pictures in your mind's eye. The right partner could be under your nose, and you might not recognize it. You may not notice this is the perfect person for you because you are not clear about what you want. Clarity in thought is needed when you seek a partner.

PICTURE YOUR PERFECT FLOWER

Don't be like a butterfly flitting from flower to flower to find what you want by trial and error. Picture your perfect flower and let it grow in the quiet of your mind. Your unconscious will guide you to the garden gate; you will recognize it when you arrive. Like Juanita, you may be in the same room with your perfect partner right now and not know it.

Your Turn

"We have what we seek, it is there all the time, and if we give it time, it will make itself known to us" (Thomas Merton).

When you are aware of how you have been programmed by the past, you are free to reprogram your dreams. Picture what you want based on love for yourself and others; and then say, write, or even sing what you want often. In the brain, *practice makes permanent.*

Juanita's statements and intentions reflect her personal and spiritual values.

- I thank God for my ideal relationship.
- I thank God for inner peace.
- I thank God for my life of joy, love, and miracles.

It also helped her to picture her dream: Juanita visualized a religious ceremony with her perfect partner on a serene lake.

You need to repeat statements of intention as often as possible. Say them, sing them, write them, and live them!

Juanita kept track of her intentions and meaningful questions on a daily basis in a journal. This is how she tracked her deepest thoughts and values.

These statements help reprogram your brain and invite the help of your higher self through your unconscious. She did not decide who her ideal partner would be. She did not say, "I thank God for my perfect relationship with Mr. Smith." Rather, she considered her purpose and her values and trusted God to guide her to her ideal relationship. Her perfect relationship was there all the time.

It was important for Juanita to let God illuminate what was right for her. It is not loving for us to decide that we want a certain person when that may not be what is best for him or her.

I have seen too many clients try to squeeze what they want out of a love relationship that does not honor the other. This always ends in failure. It is like repeatedly throwing yourself against a brick wall. The wall does not move.

I once had a professor who explained that a good relationship is like holding a bar of soap in an open hand. If you try to hold it too tight and squeeze, it will turn into a mess. In friendship on fire, there is a mutual commitment.

RECORDING SPARKS

Keeping a journal is an integral tool for friendship on fire to do the following:

➤ Blow off steam
➤ Look at patterns over time
➤ Get to know yourself
➤ Write down life lessons
➤ Write statements of intention
➤ Keep inspirational phrases
➤ Keep track of progress
➤ Look at a situation from a different perspective
➤ Take time out to calm down

Light Your Path

In 2004, a friend gave me a copy of *The 5 Year Journal* developed by Doreene Clement, which has been an invaluable resource for me. After I received *The Journal*, I was so impressed by the format that I contacted Ms. Clement, and we wrote an article together. At the time, she was working on a book called *Blessings* during a long remission from cancer. Doreene was indeed a blessing to everyone who knew her, a loving and giving spirit. She died in 2006 but her legacy remains. With permission, I have reprinted her reflections on using *The Journal* that you can order at *www.the5yearjournal.com*.

Your Turn

Keeping a Relationship Journal
By Doreene Clement and Linda Miles, Ph.D.

Keeping a relationship journal or diary for five years is an amazing, yet simple tool that supports and enhances you, your partner and your relationship. With your relationship journal, you both learn, and empower. Within the pages of your journal you will learn about yourself and your relationship. And you will begin to observe and recognize what you want to do differently, because it no longer works for you.

When you write your thoughts and experiences in a journal, you can actually see what you are thinking, putting your thoughts into a solid, tangible form. Patterns of thinking and doing, that we all have, are easily observed when recorded on paper. Creating a written record, over five years, helps to track and record life daily, writing about where we are, where we were, and especially where we want to go. Journals are a proven, effective method for personal growth that help focus, clarify, and reduce stress.

Using an already formatted book like *The 5 Year Journal* (www. the5yearjournal.com) is an easy way to keep your relationship journal. You can also use a computer, or a blank book or notebook with enough pages to record daily for five years. Each page needs to have enough room to write three lines per day, for five years.

Every day, on one line, succinctly journal your summarized answer to each of the three following questions:

1. What is most important to you about today?
2. What lesson did you learn today?
3. What affirmation or goal do you have for one year from today?

Examples

1. Today I saw myself changing for the much better.
2. I learned the difference between needs and needy.
3. I am healthy physically, mentally, emotionally, spiritually and financially.

Journaling Tips

Keep a separate journal from your partner, but decide ahead of time if you want to share your entries with each other, or if you want to keep your journals private.

You can change your mind about whether to share or keep your journal entries private.

You may start your journal on any day of the year.

Set your journal where you see it every day: On the kitchen table, your desk, or in your briefcase. This will help remind you to journal daily.

Keep a pen or pencil with your journal.

Skipping days is a part of journaling.

You can use the same color of pen or use different colors. You can also designate colors of pens for certain feelings, i.e., green = growth, blue = sadness, orange = joy, red = anger—you get the idea. If you are using the different colored pens, write in the front of your journal what you decided each color signifies.

Relationship journals are an easy, fun, and interesting way to discover more about ourselves and each other.

Where were you a year ago?
What were you doing 2 years ago?
What were you feeling 3 years ago?
What were your dreams 5 years ago?
Journal daily the next 5 years in minutes a day with
The 5 Year Journal
www.the5yearjournal.com

SHINE A LIGHT ON YOUR LIFE

Doreen Clement was a light in the lives of many; her loving continence survives through her writing. I have found journaling to be an invaluable aid to clients as they shine a light on their lives to examine behavior and choices in order to learn lessons and put their dreams into words.

THE 5 YEAR JOURNAL
Doreene Clement's Reflections

I see The New Millennium as an opportunity;
A new start, a new beginning, a continuation,
so many possibilities for all of us.
We are here at this time, within this experience
of the turn of The Century.
We are here at The Ultimate New Year of New Years.

For me, Journalizing is remembering.

To accurately and honestly remember the subtle details of personal and emotional experiences, I like to write them down. Writing makes what I want to express more solid. It allows me to be more aware and conscious. It helps me to not only visualize, but I feel a sense of release and relief after writing.

I sometimes discount my accomplishments, not always giving to myself, the support and recognition of what I've actually achieved and to what degree. Through the years friends have supported and reminded me of my successes and accomplishments, but my particular personal slant sometimes discounts my own growth, gain, and success. This is one reason I started to write, to Journal my life.

Through Journals I learned that I am usually doing better than the credit I give to myself. I can easily stop myself from going into a negative binge. I use my Journal to remember how much of a tool and advantage that hindsight can be.

Another reason I started to write in Journals was because there is something that happens after I write about my thoughts, feelings, and experiences. It helps me to understand and even let go of my thoughts and experiences more easily. Writing helps to free my mind—and focus. I am more creative and can create and hold new thoughts more easily, because I have made the room in my mind and with my time. Writing helps me to heal.

I have learned not to live in my past experiences. I now reflect for lessons rather than dwell in the past. I can now use the past as a resource. I have even problem-solved and invented in my dreams, waking in the middle of the night to record my dreams and ideas.

On the days when I make a list of "things to do," it organizes what I want to accomplish for the day—and it organizes me. It organizes my thoughts and focuses my direction. The things I have to do may change. I can leave something off the list, or not get to some of the items, but it is all written down. Nothing gets lost. There is a focus, and my tasks are made solid. As I finish each task, I cross it off my list, gaining the feeling that I have accomplished my goals. I have created successes, some large and some small, but successes all.

Journalizing does the same for my thoughts and emotions. I make a list of where I've been, what I'm feeling, and what I'm doing. I itemize through the writing—where I am, what my fears are, what I'm happy about. I create a current and ongoing truthful inventory of me.

My journalizing helps me remember to remember. I can change my mind. I can feel differently. I can make mistakes. Right then and there—when it was written down—that was where I was at. Through the years, I have come to know myself better. I have come to accept more of myself. I have learned and am learning still. I have gained, and I can say I have changed and can change some more. I know these facts about myself because I kept a record.

Through the years I've received and bought beautiful Journals—leather bound with wonderful papers. Yet some of my thoughts would end up on scraps of paper. I like ease and convenience so I decided to organize my writing—and create a method to write in—so I designed The 5 YEAR JOURNAL™.

FIRE OF CONNECTION

The love which I thought was a joke and a plaything ... it is only now that I understand it is the molder of one's life, the most solemn and sacred of all things.

—Sir Arthur Conan Doyle

Introduction
To Fire Of Connection

From the desert I came to thee, On a stallion shod with fire; and the winds are left behind in the speed of my desire.

—Bayard Taylor

Jungian analyst Marion Woodman describes the first time she saw her husband free of her own projections after years of marriage. She heard him rattling around in the kitchen attempting to poach an egg. At first, she began to think in terms of her "shoulds" and became judgmental of his inadequacy in the kitchen. She let go of all judgment and saw him for himself for the first time, standing on spindly legs in Bermuda shorts, holding an imperfect poached egg. As she watched him, she said that she felt profound love.

TRANSFORM GRUDGES INTO CREATIVE ENERGY

It can be difficult to transform grudges and judgments into creative energy, yet this practice is essential for friendship on fire.

Those with friendship on fire accept one another as is. They do not believe in the fairy tale of the perfect person, but instead live a reality tale.

Fire-of-connection cases in this section describe couples who learn to transform conflict into wisdom and compassion.

Louis Armstrong sang, "Love, baby, love—that's the secret . . . If lots more of us loved each other, we'd solve lots more problems. And then this world would be a gasser."

Fire of connection couples transform conflict into creative solutions using their artistry to

> ➢ tend their own sparks instead of getting burned, trying to manage your partner's fire,
> ➢ keep the flames alive while taking time to repair conflicts,
> ➢ balance the powerful forces of love with friendship,
> ➢ learn to avoid power struggles,
> ➢ experience intimacy in the present moment,
> ➢ share many daily acts of love,
> ➢ avoid intimidation,
> ➢ deal with life challenges as a team,
> ➢ keep the sizzle alive,
> ➢ maintain a sense of underlying oneness,
> ➢ exchange gift love instead of need love,
> ➢ avoid behaviors that can burn out connection,
> ➢ celebrate life on a daily basis,
> ➢ develop a partnership with possibility, and
> ➢ do what kindles the most love in their relationship.

"Where there is love, there is peace; where there is peace there is God" (Leo Tolstoy).

Just by holding hands with a partner and by protecting one another from the physical and mental stresses of life's hardships, you can calm down the stress response in the brain and ease health problems through love.

Jim Coan of the University of Virginia identified "supercouples" through his research who can literally buffer one another from the stress and pain of an electrical shock.

Couples with friendship on fire experience lower levels of stress. The lyrics of the Marvin Gaye rock song, "When I get this feeling, I need sexual healing," turns out to be true after all.

On the other hand, couples in the brain imaging studies by Naomi Eisenberger at the University of California have shown that rejection and exclusion trigger the same brain circuits as physical pain. Researcher Louise

Hawkley of the University of Chicago asserts that loneliness raises blood pressure, and the risk of heart attack and stroke is doubled.

We are playing with fire when we are careless with love. Learning to manage the tension between passionate expression and self-control opens the door to a friendship on fire. We need to harness these forces for the good of one another and the world.

Learning By Example

Laura was a middle-aged woman with a lasting and loving marriage to Ken. Her parents were strong models of a *friendship on fire*. As a child, she shared a bedroom with her sister, and her bed happened to be next to the wall of her parents' bedroom. Most nights, she went to sleep to the sound of her parents' laughter. While her parents did not hang a Do Not Disturb sign on their bedroom door, they often locked the door, and the two sisters would not dream of disturbing them when the door was locked. They sensed that these were special times their parents cherished. On their anniversary and occasionally on weekends, their parents would hire a babysitter and go to a motel.

JOYFUL INTIMACY

When Laura was a teenager, she saw that after many years of marriage, her parents still shared a joyful intimacy. She realized that many couples, parents of her friends, did not have such a playful and loving connection. Inspired by her parents' model, she sought a relationship that would emulate it; and, having met a caring man named Ken who was both interesting and willing to commit himself to her, she set out to develop a friendship on fire.

THE CANVAS OF INTIMACY

Think of an intimate relationship as a canvas, and you are the artists. Laura and Ken created a world with their senses, playful and alive. When their relationship became sexual, they had already co-created a canvas of joy, love, and connection.

THE BEST SEX

Research has shown great sex happens most often with safety and commitment. Mature loving is based on trust, acceptance, and a willingness to renew your life together. There is a level of comfort, reassurance, and mutual satisfaction.

Masters and Johnson referred to good sex as "two children under the sheets." In order to have this kind of physical intimacy, you must be able to let go and relax. Orgasm is about letting go; and there are so many kinds of intimacy, some without orgasm, that couples may enjoy as they revisit familiar modes of connection and discover still more ways to please one another.

Discovering what you and your partner can offer each other in the way of pleasure takes time, patience, and trust. If your partner is your best friend, you will be able to commit yourself in ways that make your mutual pleasure both more lasting and intense.

RISKY VENTURES

If you choose to become intimate with a stranger, there is no commitment. The pleasure you have may be momentarily intense, but it is fleeting, and the consequences may be whoppers. Momentary pleasure is often fraught with anxiety not only with regard to risks, but also with regard to the desires of the uncommitted partner that is the only connecting bond.

PAUNCH PROBLEMS

Physical defects that committed lovers overlook or even regard with affection—paunchiness, cellulite, or signs of aging—are liable to diminish or extinguish the desire that brought you and the uncommitted lover together. Fearing this, you are bound to be preoccupied with how you look. Does he/she like my size and shape? Combine this preoccupation with performance anxiety in sex, also common with uncommitted lovers, and it is unlikely that you will be rewarded with anything comparable to the kind of pleasure enjoyed by committed lovers.

TRYING-TO-IMPRESS MODE

I often warn clients that new sexual relationships may not be like those idealized in pseudosophisticated magazines like *Cosmo* that promote promiscuity or bodice-ripping romance novels. Sex doesn't always work perfectly with a new partner. Often you are in trying-to-impress mode, which means you are not your real self and may not feel safe enough to let go. Since orgasm is about letting go, you may have to act like the young woman in *When Harry Met Sally* who gave a picture-perfect demonstration of how to fake an orgasm. You try to second-guess to impress and decide to try some new techniques, wondering if this is the right thing to do with this new partner.

CONNECTION THROUGH AFFECTION

In friendship on fire, sex is defined as connection through affection. Even a kiss on the mouth can spark such connection. Our lips are very sensitive organs and can work like glue for bonding.

Those with friendship on fire do not stop the long and loving kisses after courtship. *The American Heritage Dictionary* defines a kiss as "an expression of greeting, respect or amorousness." In order to retain friendship on fire, we need connection, mutual respect, and affection.

It is no accident that the phrase "kiss off" means "go away," "disrespect," and "contempt." This book also aims to help you avoid such unfortunate endings.

What are the secrets to friendship on fire? How can you recognize couples who retain the kind of loving and lasting union? If you did not have positive role models, look for some. They may be paunchy, over sixty, or using a walker; but you will recognize them by their passionate and joyful tactics. Even Forest Gump could spot these couples and knew life could be like a box of chocolates.

Gerald Jampolsky cautions us to "be a love-finder rather than a fault-finder." Look for moments to offer love.

Your Turn

Spend time with your partner, stroking one another and identifying ways you make each other feel safe to be who you are to explore your sexuality. Share what you enjoy most. Great sex begins with two people who want to please one another.

With *friendship on fire*, both partners are givers. One-way streets get old. Talk to your lover. During and between encounters, tell him/her how lucky you feel to have them. Tell them how good they look to you. "You're still hot" is an old line, but said with feeling, it resonates.

If you have problems with letting go, practice some of the mindfulness techniques in this book to help you relax and enjoy the moment. Identify ways you can strengthen your friendship, and have more fun when you are sexually intimate.

1. Do you and your partner call or text one another with playful and sexual innuendo?
2. Are you able to be playful sexually?
3. Do you connect with one another emotionally during sex?
4. Are you able to openly share desires and fantasies?
5. Are you able to stay in the present moment as you pleasure one another?
6. Do you make time for affectionate gestures?
7. Identify at least three ways to share affection.
8. Identify at least three ways you remain lovers for life despite daily demands. Even small gestures are like an emotional bank account that adds up over time.

Fire Management After An Affair

Roberta and Jack came for their first appointment in crisis. Roberta reported that she was jolted awake by a phone call late on Thursday night while Jack was away at a business conference. The caller identified himself as the husband of one of Jack's female co-workers and informed her that their two spouses were having an affair. Roberta stayed awake the rest of the night desperately trying to text or page her husband. He did not answer. The next day after she dropped the three children at school she got cell phone records and read Jack's E-mail. She made copies of graphic E-mails leading up to the conference when the two co-workers exchanged explicit sexual conversations. She was enraged and then collapsed in tears after the children were in bed.

EMOTIONAL MAELSTROM

Jack walked into a maelstrom of emotions. Roberta lashed out from extreme hurt, anger and feelings of betrayal. When Jack attempted to deny his involvement she crazily grabbed the E-Mails and began to read graphic sections.

Roberta reported that the rest of the week-end was a blur and that she had not eaten and slept very little. Jack declared his love for Roberta and she sarcastically whispered, "Yeah, right".

THE KEY QUESTIONS

The most important things I needed to establish in the first session were:

1. Would Jack give up the other woman so they could work on the marriage?
2. Did Roberta want to remain committed to Jack?
3. Would they commit to working on their issues in an authentic way?
4. Could Jack be compassionate about Roberta's feelings of betrayal?

After we made agreements on these four questions I began to gather history. Both partners had deep issues that they needed to face. Jack had problems with self-judgements and felt devalued after they had children and Roberta paid little attention to him. When his co-worker came on to him, he felt desirable and his ego was bolstered.

Roberta felt neglected as a child and wanted to spare her children this pain so she became too child centered. She was unaware that Jack felt devalued.

MISTAKES ARE TEACHERS

It is important to forgive and learn from mistakes in relationships. If you want friendship on fire, you need to be able to handle flames of crisis. Affairs are exceedingly tough because of feelings of betrayal and trust issues. These take time and commitment to heal. Forgiveness does not mean forgetfulness so this couple needed to agree that affairs were off limits. Jack needed to demonstrate his strong commitment and loyalty to Roberta over time.

Although Jack's affair was a destructive choice for this couple they were able to empathize with one another's pain. They made many changes including increased affection, connection and protection. Over time the trust returned. I ran into Jack many years later in a parking lot and he shared pictures of grandchildren with tears in his eyes. He thanked me for helping his wife see he was really a good man and capable of change.

Your Turn:

If either of you have had an affair ask yourselves the four questions. If the answers are yes then your relationship can start on the road to recovery.

If either of you remains uncommitted, give your decisions time and thought. Try not to make final decisions in the midst of a crisis. Take some time ask the questions together and educate yourself about potential consequences of ending the relationship.

Keeping the Flame Alive

Accustom yourself continually to make many acts of love, for they enkindle and melt the soul.

—Saint Teresa of Avila

If you want a behavior to become permanent, you *need to* practice it on a regular basis. I have seen countless couples who think that "it" will just happen without realizing that the "it" is them. April and Jackson were such a couple. Although both were hard working, can-do types, after they married, they expected things to "just happen" in their relationship. When April complained that "it is just not the same between us," I asked her to define "it." After a moment of confusion, she smiled and said," Well, I guess it must refer to us." This was the beginning of change.

MIND TRAPS

As long as this couple was trapped in passivity, the light of their connection was dim. They needed to develop a clear intention to change. According to Dr. Daniel Siegel in his book *The Mindful Brain*, "We have words and ideas that frame and form the field of awareness and dull our senses . . . But the real truth is that those cognitive contraptions help structure a neural attempt to make sense of a complex world, only to then entrap us in the very structures that we have created." The word "it" is a mind trap.

As April and Jackson began to practice loving behaviors, they began to permanently wire that sequence of neurons into their brains. Over time, the neural pathways became habitual since in the brain, "practice makes permanent."

"Neurons that wire together fire together" (Donald Hebb). The links of associations that we make are reactivated in the future.

MIRROR NEURONS

> Stay together, friends.
> Don't scatter and sleep.
> Our friendship is made.
> Of being awake. (Rumi)

Loving behavior needs to be practiced to maintain a rewarding and lasting relationship. Each of us may express and experience love in different ways throughout our lives. We have brain cells called mirror neurons that allow us to reflect the feelings of another and feel empathy for them by giving us a chance to walk in his/her shoes. Through these neuronal pathways, we attune to the other person. Daniel Siegel notes that through attunement, two separate elements are brought into a "resonating whole."

"NEURONS THAT WIRE TOGETHER FIRE TOGETHER"

The more you practice understanding the reality of others, the stronger these connections become. This explains why loving and lasting couples maintain a *friendship on fire*. They get one another, live in the present moment, and see elements of an ordinary day as magical through a shared love of life. Theirs is, as Sade sings of it, "No ordinary love."

In the Song of Songs in the Bible, the unnamed lover (believed to be God) watches us from behind the scenery of our everyday world. If we are stuck in our own mind traps, we do not see the joy, love, and miracles splashed across our lives. Love and acceptance are lenses through which we can see the graceful present.

Your Turn

Ask yourself the following questions:

- Do I wait for "it" to change?

- What prevents me from staying in the present moment?
- What kinds of mind traps keep me stuck (e.g., "it" traps, fear of change, guilt over past actions, unresolved anger)?
- How can I begin to focus on a new intention to experience love and grace in the present moment?

You can invite your thoughts to show up and look at them without judgment through a practice of mindfulness. Your thoughts mean to protect you. Just observe them; they may have helped you survive in the past. Mindfulness is about making your mind spacious to allow for acceptance and transformation. "Nothing is intentionally blocked; rather all guests are welcome" (Dan Siegel).

The following practice can help you become more aware of your mind. Limit your practice to five or ten minutes at times when you are not too stressed. You can do it several times a day.

Begin by focusing on your breathing. Count seven very deep breaths in your mind, breathing deeply. Become aware of you stomach. It may feel very tight from holding tension of the ego. See if you can let some of that tension flow away, and loosen the muscles in your midsection. Notice other tension in you body, not judging, just observing.

Soften your eyes so your gaze is gentle. Allow your mind to open—relaxed yet spontaneous. Picture an ocean, and let your awareness blend with that boundless space. Allow thoughts and emotions to arise and dissolve in the ocean.

Follow your breath into a tranquil place. Notice the sounds around you, allowing thoughts and emotions to arise and disperse into the vast ocean. Just take note of sensations in your body and thoughts. You mind may wander; just come back to breathing gently and lovingly.

Your mind is like a huge body of water, boundless enough to allow thoughts to liquefy endlessly. Take three more deep breaths, and return to your regular activities.

There is quite a bit of research now available on the efficacy of this kind of practice for a sense of well-being and ability to live in the present moment. You will realize at a deep level that "it" is you.

Birthday Candles

When I first saw April and Jackson, it was because of a terrible argument they had about her birthday. In April's family, birthdays were big deals; they were one of the ways that April's parents showed their love for her.

Jackson grew up in a family that did not celebrate birthdays because of religious beliefs. His parents showed their love through daily caretaking and making sure that the family was provided for. His father brought his mother coffee in bed nearly every morning. She often cooked his favorite dishes.

TRAIN WRECKS

The first year April and Jackson were together, her birthday was a giant train wreck. When Jackson did not arrange for any celebrations or gifts, she thought he didn't love her and that she needed to cut her losses by breaking up.

Jackson was clueless and blown away by April's freak-out and threats to end the relationship. He ran out to get flowers at the grocery store, which much to his dismay only seemed to make matters worse.

WHAT MATTERS MOST

It is important to avoid the "I'm right; you're wrong" posturing that brought April and Jackson to see me. We all grow up under different circumstances that condition our thoughts and behaviors. Couples like April and Jackson need to learn about one another, and this can bring conflict. These kinds of conflicts are part of an important phase of a relationship when you are learning what matters most to your partner. Couples that take a lazy or blaming approach to this phase wind up with more disruptions.

Initially, this couple became more agitated when Jackson failed to see the emotional importance and blamed April, "You're making a big fat deal over nothing."

April responded, "You're just an insensitive jerk," which, of course, only brought more snags into the mix.

STOP THE "IT" WORD

After attending therapy sessions and working on the reasons behind their reactions to April's birthday, they began to learn more about what was important to the other. They stopped using the "it" word when referring to their problems, and Jackson understood although it was not logical to him that birthdays were celebrations of love to her. For April, it was important to learn what made Jackson feel cared for and to get that he did not intend to discount her with his words. He was using logic when he did get her emotional picture.

TRIAL AND ERROR

This trail-and-error phase of relationships follows the romantic phase, so this is the time when those with friendship on fire figure out what matters most.

The next year, Jackson made sure there was a celebration, and April worked on being aware of how important daily meals together were for him.

All couples have train wrecks because of people, places, habits, events from the past. You are a product of how you were raised, how you were treated, and what you experienced. You learn from others around you. You base your decisions on what to do and how to act and interact on your past experiences and social mores of the earlier places in your life.

TODAY IS A DIFFERENT DAY

Today is different from what went before. This couple used mindfulness practice to help them become aware of how they were conditioned by the past. Together they decided what was important to keep and what precedents could go.

WHAT LOVE MEANS FOR YOU

The most important part is learning about the other person and learning to practice what love means for each of you. This helps you develop celebrations and rituals that honor both.

Your Turn

If you are single, write down five behaviors of friends or loved ones that make you feel loved or special. Recognize that there are more behaviors that can make you feel loved, but the ones you have listed will give you a better idea of what you would like to see in your next relationship. Get a loved one involved; ask them about your behaviors and what you have done for them that made them feel special or loved.

If you are currently in a relationship, list five behaviors that your partner can do that make you feel loved. Make an agreement with one another to practice these behaviors for and with each other as often as possible. You can practice simple things on a daily basis.

On a scale of one to ten, how high is your commitment to one another?

If you score low, discuss what goals you need to set to develop stronger commitments to one another. Identify three ways to achieve your intentions. Keep up the discussions; communication is essential if you hope to achieve them. Give it your best effort, and remember that it will take several months to reach a higher level of commitment.

Even if your relationship eventually ends, you will feel better if you know you gave it your best effort.

Some ways you can strengthen your commitment to each other:

- Make connections with your eyes, voice, and body language.
- Practice mindfulness so you can remain in the present with your partner.
- Find humor in everyday things. Remember laughter is connected with bonding.

- Build an emotional bank account. At the end of each day, share one thing you appreciate about the other. These add up over time and improve your sense of commitment.
- Don't just survive—visualize. Close your eyes and imagine how you *want* your relationship to be. Get the focus off what you do not want.
- Wake up without makeup. Be authentic with your partner.
- Share grown-up sex. Grown-up sex is not about hooking up with but looking up at your partner and loving that person with knobby knees, cellulite, or well-earned wrinkles. Accept the real person instead of wishing he was airbrushed, or she was the *Playboy* centerfold.
- You cannot stop life's sorrows, but you can choose joy. Recall your best bad day; do not catch your partner's bad moods. Inoculate yourself with your own protective shield of humor.

Rekindle Love Daily

Stan and Megan were both forty-five and had been married twenty years; they had two teenage daughters. Each year, they took a two-week vacation to some special place. They loved to travel and have incredible memories from the trips. However, at home their lives were stressful and negative. Like many couples, they waited until they went away to have a good time.

Why wait? You miss out on many little things each day that can add up to making a positive difference in your relationship.

BANK ACCOUNT OF LOVE

Little moments add up to a good relationship. Each time you or your partner smiles, touches, winks, or makes jokes, you make a deposit in the bank account of love. The account grows each time you make a contribution. It is not a yearly two-week vacation that makes a difference; it is the daily things: sharing a hug while watching TV, enjoying a cup of hot chocolate together on a cold evening, or laughing about things together.

LAUGHTER IS A LANGUAGE OF CONNECTION

Laughter is an important language of connection. It is the emotional cement that bonds families together. Those who have friendship on fire share a sense of humor.

They laugh about things and enjoy recollecting moments in their history together that may have been stressful and anything but humorous—an emergency dealt with, an embarrassment—but viewed in retrospect begets laughter.

Parents and children have always gotten to know one another through tickles, games, and playful exchanges. Laughter is healthy; as the saying goes, "Laughter is the best medicine."

LAUGHING AT YOURSELF

Years ago a dear friend discovered the power of laughter for connecting with others. She was a new hire of a huge computer corporation—one of the first woman hires and the only female in her training class. The first day she was a wreck but dressed for success in an expensive suit and high heels. She did a great imitation of someone who knew what she was doing until it was time to get off the trainee transport. She gracefully stood, confidently walked past all the guys, and proceeded to fall off the steps of the bus.

Her tumble broke the ice for the whole group as several guys came to her aid. Once they found out she was OK, everyone, including the woman, had a good laugh over the incident. Our human flaws endear us to others.

Your Turn

Look back at your past and rekindle your relationship feelings:

- What did you do for fun when you first got together? What little things did you enjoy when you developed your relationship and have stopped doing over time?
- What things did you do to make the sparks fly?
- Ask each other what about the little things that meant so much in the beginning and use them to rekindle the warm embers.
- Discuss ways that you and your partner can enjoy more of the little things in the moment.

You can train your brain to be more peaceful and joyful. Try to practice alone or as a couple. Close your eyes and imagine a beautiful, peaceful place. Maybe it is the mountains, maybe the beach. Go there in your mind. See, listen, touch. When you open your eyes, take a moment and focus your attention on an object in the room—perhaps a plant, part of a painting, a pillow, the way light filters through the curtains.

Gradually you can train your brain to slow down and focus on the present. If your mind wanders off, you bring it back over and over again if necessary. Acknowledge the things for which you are grateful. Begin to train your brain to focus on the gifts that surround you. Tell yourself, "I am grateful for peace and tranquility."

This practice will help you remain centered in the present moment. As you train your mind to avoid judgment and appreciate the now, you will loosen up and begin to experience humor. Our ego keeps us stuck in past or future evaluations, and we lose the precious moment.

THE KEY QUESTIONS

Raymond Moody, M.D., studied stories of people who had near-death experiences. Many people on the edge of death focused on two questions. What wisdom have I gained from this life? How did I expand my capacity to love? I could relate when I read his work since I had a near-death experience and have a similar deep knowing that the meaning of my life was measured in moments of love.

Practice being present in the moment, express gratitude, and develop the wisdom to be a better person every day.

"Life is this simple. We are living in a world that is absolutely transparent and the divine is shining through all the time. This is not just a nice story or a fable. This is true" (Thomas Merton).

If you would like some help with your mindfulness practice, go to www. drlindamiles.com for a CD that will provide you with more guidance.

The Shared Flame

Alexandra and Mark were mired in shame-and-blame games. Although they loved each other very much, they had no idea how to break this destructive cycle.

"WE" STATEMENTS

I recommended that they use "we" instead of "I" when they discussed a problem.

Although "I" statements can be helpful if you take turns speaking and listening, they can also be used as weapons. For example, Alexandra began sentences by saying, "I think *you* are very selfish"; and Mark would shoot back, "I break my neck for this family, and *you* don't seem to notice." This attack mode of blaming, accusing, or shaming was destroying their relationship.

There is an old expression that if you want a good relationship you need to turn "Me" upside down and make it "WE".

MORE JUDGMENT, LESS LOVE

"The more one judges, the less one loves" (Honoré de Balzac).

Blaming is bound to generate hostility because the one blamed feels resentful and bound to defend himself/herself. It's hard to feel love for someone who is shaming you even if you know that you and that person love each other. Blame and shame can only drive people apart. There is no point in an endless cycle of shame and blame.

I asked them to phrase the question, "How can *we* do a better job of meeting each other's needs?"

THE THIRD ENTITY

As we discussed earlier, Pierre Teilhard de Chardin emphasized that *three* parties were involved in a marriage. Two were the bride and the groom, and the third was "the baby," or the marriage itself. Be sure never to lose sight of that third entity in your relationship.

Many people do not consider the "we-ness" in their relationship and drop "the baby" on its head. As the old saying goes, "Don't throw the baby out with the bath water." *Friendship on fire* means that you make your relationship a priority. The child of your combined hearts needs attention and warmth.

Your Turn

Think about how you can resolve problems by using the word "we" instead of attacking one another. Do you have any unresolved issues where you are tempted to blame your partner? Try making it a problem where "we" is needed. This puts you both on the same team.

For example, ask "How can we handle this disagreement about money in a constructive way?" instead of saying, "I hate it when you sneak around and spend money behind my back."

After you have an argument or find yourselves shouting at one another, once you have calmed down, review what you could have done better by using the "we" approach and see how you can better resolve the problem.

Intimidation is Incendiary

Sticks and stones may break my bones, but words can break my soul.
—Sarah Rogers

After a talk I gave on relationships in a bookstore, Sarah came up from the audience and explained that she was a songwriter and wanted to write a song about intimidation tactics. She said she had already decided on a title, "Sticks and Stones May Break My Bones, but Words Can Break My Soul." Months later, a surprise package arrived containing a CD that included this song. I was touched to hear Sarah's beautiful voice, helping others to recognize the powerful effect of words.

Sarah wrote several songs about the pain of verbal abuse. She describes the accumulation of emotionally abusive scars and how these scars destroy a relationship.

INTIMIDATION TACTICS

Intimidation tactics are power plays designed to control your partner's behavior. Even if you win the battle, you ultimately lose the war because you kill off pieces of your connection. "The fire you kindle for your enemy often burns you more than him" (Chinese proverb). Intimidation tactics that break the bonds of a relationship include the following but are not limited to these:

- shouting
- name-calling

- put-downs
- unfavorable comparisons
- rehashing the past for years
- slamming stuff around
- hostile silence
- global versus specific criticism
- staring like a snake
- eye rolling

CHEMICAL COCKTAILS

Couples who don't respect each other are like explosive Molotov cocktails. Not only do bad feelings linger in the air, but such couples also suffer internally. Negative chemical cocktails are released from the adrenal glands when home fires are out of control. "Hating people is like burning down your own house to get rid of a rat" (Harry Fosdick).

The chemical storm starts when the brain sends out a distress signal that jump-starts a chain reaction, which, in turn, raises your blood pressure. You become a boiling pot, which starts you down the path toward heart disease or depression.

CHOOSE LIFE OVER LIP

If you allow anger, fear, or other negative thoughts instead of love to guide your decisions, you may be at *more* risk for poor physical and mental health, poverty, loneliness, and earlier death. Anger and fear are often caused by a lack of belief in yourself and feeling that you do not deserve better. Fear in bad relationships often manifests itself as hostility, jealousy, and shame.

MOUTHING OFF

If you are mired in such mouthing-off behaviors, ask yourself if this is how you want to live your life. "You can preach a better sermon with your life than with your lips" (Oliver Goldsmith).

USE GENTLE TO EXPRESS STRONG

A proverb tells us to "use gentle to express strong." When we whisper, people strain to listen because of increased neural activity in the listener's brain. Think of Clint Eastwood as he said, "Make my day" at a very low volume. Those with friendship on fire are generally able to just say no, or when the fire is too hot, they know how to stop and repair.

Intimidation Tactics	Constructive Alternatives
Staring at your partner with snake eyes	Attacking weeds in the yard
Yelling	Expressing strong feelings with a kind and firm voice
Rehashing the past	Using awareness practice to focus on the present moment
Hostile silence	Using centering prayer—repeating a spiritual word like "love," "God," or "peace" to refocus your mind on love and kindness

Your Turn

Think of the times you have used intimidation tactics. Even though that tactic gets you what you want at the time, it can have a long-term influence on the relationship, and you will pay a price for your behavior. If the intimidation tactics continue, eventually, a bell will sound in one of your heads; one of you is ready to cash in on the relationship. Do not accumulate negative points. *Friendship on fire* is built on positive points and problem solving.

How do you or your partner use intimidation tactics? Make a list, and then consider constructive alternatives. Identify your own problem behaviors and commit to constructive alternatives. Refrain from shame and blame. If you and your partner cannot discuss this constructively, then clean up your act and refuse to engage in behaviors that damage your souls. If you allow abusive behavior, you also keep your partner mired in destructiveness. You never do something to someone else that you are not also doing to yourself.

BLOCKING MEANINGFUL MOMENTS

If you choose to be mean to one another, it will block meaningful moments between you and your partner. You also wound yourself and block the growth of inner wisdom when you engage in repetitive arguments and recurring dramas.

If you allow your partner to use intimidation tactics, you compromise your integrity and help keep your partner stuck in destructive behaviors. To give or receive intimidation scorches your connection.

If either of you hits, shoves, pushes or uses any kind of physical violence, you need to get help. These behaviors and not only destructive, they are illegal. It is best to seek help individually until you can control physical violence. Most phone books have a listing for a domestic violence hotline if you feel you are in danger. There are also resources available on the internet.

Managing Friction About Children

When Laura Lee and Ron married, they had loads of time to spend in the sack, lots of spare time after work, and shared *friendship on fire*.

They were elated when Laura Lee learned she was pregnant three years later. When they brought baby Michael home, things changed. Like many new parents, they hadn't worked out a team approach to parenting before the fact and began to fight about whose turn it was to take care of Michael. Getting up in the middle of the night made both of them tired and cranky; for the first time in their marriage, they fought about sex.

Laura Lee was nursing Michael and had little time to herself. She was preoccupied bonding with Michael, and her testosterone levels were lower, which reduced her sexual desire.

THREE-WAY BONDS

Ron was jealous of the time Laura Lee spent with Michael; he wanted his wife back and was unsure of how to handle his feelings. They had not had sex for weeks, and he was still secreting the same levels of testosterone and growing increasingly frustrated. He had no idea that increased levels of oxytocin (the chemical that helps bond mother and baby) in Laura Lee's body were responsible for what he perceived as rejection; it was never covered in sex education at school or with the obstetrician.

Once Ron understood what was going on with Laura Lee's body chemistry, they planned to have three-way snuggles. Ron also agreed to feed and bathe the baby while Laura Lee relaxed. The result was she felt more like having sex. They realized that even though they were tired, they needed sexual contact because having sex generates endorphins that elevates your mood and enhances loving feelings.

Pregnancy and postpartum are stressful for both parents. Not everyone reacts the same way to these challenges in life; each couple is unique and needs to find their own approach and solutions. You need to go through the experience yourself to understand and learn how to handle it.

Although you are more aware of how hormones affect your mood at times such as childbirth, remember your brain keeps working as a chemical factory. Scientists have found that the quality of connections with others can affect your health and longevity. Human brains are plastic; like Play-Doh™, they can be molded in different ways and change throughout their lives. Although the plasticity is greatest during childhood, interactions with others continue to mold the human brain. In his book, *The Developing Mind*, Dan Siegel describes the brain as a "social organism."

When Laura Lee lashed out at or rejected her husband, she felt bad; she suffered guilt and remorse seeing how her actions influenced Ron's behavior. All those stress-related chemicals draining into her body left her down in the dumps.

Ron had to fight an urge to drink to feel better after their fights. Together they found the way back to *friendship on fire* and stoked up those healing hormones.

Couples with friendship on fire are able to expand in love for family. They are flexible in their roles and share leadership. Of course, having children adds many complications to daily lives, yet friendship-on-fire couples find ways to co-create order and discipline while filling a home with meaning and love.

I recall visiting a colleague who had five children and a friendship on fire. She and her husband were poetry in motion as they seamlessly handed the baby to one another as needed, cooked, and interacted with the other kids with gusto. Their respect and consideration for one another were reflected in their flair for childrearing.

Do not feel discouraged if you do not share this couple's knack for parenting; the point is that those with friendship on fire find a way to work as a team and spell one another when times are tough.

"The House of the Heart is never full" (African proverb).

Your Turn

Discuss ways that you can manage the stress of raising children in more positive ways so you stay on the same team. How can you both grow as people and parents in your understanding and respect for the power of love? How can you disagree and still show respect? How can you set family rules for respect, teamwork, and loving kindness? Will you be able to model friendship on fire for your children?

If you don't have children, what are the stresses in your life that generate negative chemicals that can pull you apart? What behaviors can you change that will help you generate positive chemicals? Write down what happened just before you stated feeling stressed. This can lead you to your behaviors that you need to start correcting.

Here are the ways Ron and Laura Lee managed the challenge of new baby.

- Engaged in three-way cuddles
- Gave one another alone time
- Resumed regular sexual activity based on doctor's recommendations
- Wrote down their *friendship-on-fire* behaviors and exchanged loving looks on a daily basis
- Took time-outs when they felt like shouting
- Used soft voices as much as possible around Michael
- Practiced awareness and centering prayer to deal with increased life challenges
- Listened to the reality of the other person

They also set a family-renewal time when they relaxed using a relaxation CD. They were surprised to seen how much Michael responded to the music and their peaceful mood. They then told each other something that they were grateful for in the other (children also love this as they get older).

Flare Ups

Margaret and Joel had been married for ten years and had created adjoining prison cells in their marriage based on past ideas and patterns.

Joel was the eldest of three sons; he grew up feeling unwanted and devalued by his critical parents, resulting in low self-esteem. He began building walls to keep out the hurt.

Margaret's background was similar. Her mother was critical of everything about her: hair, skin, grades, and the way she dressed. As far as Margaret was concerned, she just couldn't win. Margaret built her wall as a retreat from her greatest critic. She walled herself off, made perfect grades, and decided that if she achieved enough, her mother would accept her.

After they married, Margaret continued to push herself, often working long hours.

Joel saw Margaret's ambition as a reflection of his parents. He wanted more from Margaret; he wanted to feel valued, he wanted more attention, and he wanted to be the focus of Margaret's life. He would lose his temper about things Margaret considered silly, like talking on the phone too long or forgetting to run an errand for him. Based on decisions he made as a child, he interpreted Margaret's ambition and actions as evidence that she did not love him.

Joel and Margaret were prisoners of childhood decisions. He intended to protect himself by demanding more attention, and she attempted self-protection by working harder to achieve. What protected them as children backfired as husband and wife. Both needed to reevaluate what was in their best interest and what was best for their marriage.

REMOVING THE BRICKS

Once Joel and Margaret understood they had built walls to shut each other out because of past hurts, they began to remove bricks. They realized that they needed a different focus, not the looking glass from the past, but a vision of what their lives could be as *friendship on fire*.

WHAT YOU EXPECT

You see what you expect to see. Brain science has found that a small percentage of what we see is through our vision. Neuroscientist Richard Gregory estimates visual perception is more than 90 percent memory and less than 10 percent sensory nerve signals.

As you drive up to your house, if you see you dog running behind a picket fence to meet you, your eyes see vertical images of the dog with large slices missing, yet you perceive your whole canine buddy.

This couple needed to learn to question their perceptions since much of what they perceived was based on the past.

THOUGHTS ARE NOT SET IN STONE

What you focus on in your partner reflects your own state of mind; relationships reveal all your warts and wounds. However, your thoughts and behaviors are not set in stone; you can change them. But just like any wound, they take time to heal. There is no quick fix, no microwave solution, or a pill to make it better. The investment is worth it to bring down the walls and give yourself a chance to enjoy a *friendship on fire*.

MAP YOUR VISION

Begin to live your life by choice. Map your own vision of what you want, and don't rely on your automatic pilot. It may have worked well in the past, but now, it takes you way off course.

Set your new navigation system in the direction of your dreams. *You are the instrument of your behavior change!* Don't be too hard on yourself; remember it takes time to achieve change. Once you realize that you have been wearing old-fashioned spectacles to see the world, you can learn to question your view. Don't be so afraid of change that you use familiar routes that land you in the badlands.

Take off your spectacles, make some adjustments, refocus, and be sure that you are looking at your intended objective: your *friendship on fire*.

Your Turn

Thoughts and behaviors practiced in your family of origin become automatic. Imagine that you are looking through a pair of binoculars. Take a good look into your brain, and focus on behaviors that have been detrimental to your relationships. What were they? Are they behaviors that mirror what you learned at an earlier age? If these behaviors were practiced until they became permanent, then your brain is just trying to protect you.

Your binocular practice has six stages:

1. Question your perception of things. Expressions like "My way or the highway" are a disaster in relationships.
2. Identify two areas in your relationship that cause problems.
3. Write down your desired destination.
4. Practice looking for love and beauty.
5. Use your relationship to practice giving and receiving love.
6. If you are becoming more loving and compassionate and less explosive, you are making progress.

History Blazes a Trail

When Josh came for his first session, he wore chinos and a Chicago Bears shirt. He was a relaxed and entertaining dude who worked as a graphic artist. His wife, Jana, a fellow graphic artist, wore jeans and a trendy tee. Although both were lively and outgoing, they told me they loved one another but their relationship was *boring*. How did this happen?

COUCH POTATO CONDITIONING

Both came from couch potato families, and they unconsciously aped the boring lifestyles of their parents. Conditioned by their upbringing, they settled into the same mindless routines of sedentary indulgence and TV watching.

MIND MOVIES

Your brain follows the pictures in your mind, and you often rerun the same tape over and over again. Their brains' unconscious picture showed a boring homelife planted in front of a TV; they approached their marriage in the same way they needed a wake-up reminder since they were not living their life by choice. As Twain observed, "Loyalty to petrified opinion never yet broke a chain or freed a human soul in this world . . . and never will."

This was not how they started. Their first date was on a motorcycle trip to a rock concert, but once they married, the old familiar pictures took over. They stopped growing and were no longer interesting to each other.

LOVE IS LIFE

Love is active and brings life. Boredom is lethal. It kills relationships. People bored with each other are apt to stray, looking for the zest and excitement they have lost. So it was with Josh and Jana. Josh stopped including Jana in his adventures, and she began an affair at work. Both assumed that they had to look outside of their relationship for excitement and happiness.

CHANGE YOUR CHANNELS

Consider the models that you grew up with, and decide which are worth emulating and which are object lessons in what to avoid. When you have a friendship on fire, like those you know who might serve as models, you don't need to look for happiness in bars, titillating books and magazines, or browsing on the Internet. You can have the real thing by making sure you load the brain tape you want. Remember you are in charge of your remote; you can choose your brain channel or DVD. Return to the channels that are filled with spirit and wonder. "Go outside to the fields, enjoy nature and the sunshine, go out and recapture happiness in yourself and in God' (Anne Frank).

SAME OLD SINGSONG

Most people long for a loving and lasting union, and yet many are not sure how to make it happen. They set out with high hopes and few skills and wind up with an unrewarding relationship. They repeat patterns that failed the last generation and then become angry and distant. They *wait* for something to magically change—a new baby, a new house, or move to another city—all external things that keep them from looking inside themselves and dealing with the negative patterns they drag around.

Neither the new baby nor the new house will make the change they are hoping for; it can make things worse. New things don't keep people together; daily living and caring for one another make the relationship. New homes or new babies bring new challenges to a marriage; both mean a lot of change, and any form of change can be stressful. Despite all these changes, the same old singsong plays in your mind.

YOU OWN THE REMOTE CONTROL

Remember that there is an astonishing capability to face life challenges, and you own the remote control. Train your brain to mark favorite channels that lead to purpose and love.

As neuroscientist, Joseph LeDoux observes in his book, *The Emotional Brain*, "Psychotherapy is just another way to rewire your brain." I have used the following exercise many times for those who are stuck on negative brain channels.

Your Turn

Take a few moments to relax and close your eyes. In your mind's eye, picture a giant television screen. Notice what you are thinking, and imagine those words or images on the screen. How does it feel when you watch those words or images on the screen? Notice the reaction in your body.

Now imagine that you have a changer in your hand and that you can change to a channel with a peaceful, healing scene—maybe the beach, maybe the mountains. See what you see, hear what you hear, and notice how your body feels as you watch these words or images.

When the channel changes in your mind, just notice what words or images appear—just notice—and then practice changing the channel to the peaceful place in your mind.

Now take a moment and picture a time when you felt joyful and fully alive. Notice the sensations in your body as you respond to the picture in your mind.

Remember that you are more than your thoughts; put them outside of you so you are the observer, and simply watch and change channels when you want. With practice, your ability to flip channels will increase.

If you are like Josh and Jana, you also need to think about how you might be holding yourself back from the fun and loving relationship of your dreams.

Do you recall when you first fell in love? Describe your behavior and that of your partner. Write it down and read it repeatedly. You will bring back the feelings and emotions from when you met your partner.

Too often, long-term relationship partners stop the very behaviors that connected them with one another. Things like

- looking deeply into one another's eyes;

- concentrating on one another;
- complimenting each other with words, gifts, etc.

Write down what behaviors connected you in your relationship and then answer the following questions:

- What has your partner stopped doing?
- What have you stopped doing?
- What behaviors would you like to restore to your relationship?
- When are you going to start on your new path to restoring your relationship?
- How do you intend to accomplish your new goals?

CHANNELS OF CHOICE

As a psychotherapist, I have often referred to Anthony Ryle, who observed that the purpose of psychotherapy is to expand your ability to live your life by choice. Pick up your remote control and find your channels of choice.

Fire Watches

When Sylvia and Raul came for their first therapy session, I was quite surprised when Sylvia took out a long typed list and proceeded to read complaints about Raul.

After the first five complaints, I stopped her. "I want to help you to solve your problems as a couple and not take sides."

They told me that their previous therapist had requested the list-making, which infuriated Raul. He felt as if he was being ganged up on each week.

SCOREKEEPERS

Raul and Sylvia had not learned to work on things together and were not able to get past shaming and blaming. Each counted up the times the other did things they didn't like, but then never talked about it. They were scorekeepers. They waited, watched, and counted.

Too many partners keep a list of one another's offenses in their head. Lists can be useful to track what needs to be done around the house or what is needed from the grocery store. Adding up each thing that your partner does and then using that against him/her fuels fires of hostility. When you perceive things are wrong, your partner won't know unless you discuss them in a calm and adult manner.

Don't rely on telepathy. Don't wait; procrastination will not make things better. Face up to your concerns, and talk about them. Pick a time that will work for both of you. Don't try to do it when your partner arrives home from work or when their favorite program is about to start on TV!

TALLYING UP MISTAKES

Unfortunately, people in relationships often spend too much tim watching their partner and counting up perceived mistakes. If that is wha you are looking for, you will certainly find plenty to justify negative behavior Remember, if you are behaving that way, your partner could be doing th same thing to you. Stop adding up the mistakes and start talking.

Do not be like folks who follow fires and stand by and watch as their partners self-destruct. Rather, consider that you are guardians of you spiritual fire. Remember the power of this fire and do all that you can to use it for good.

Your Turn

Are you a watcher? Do you need to communicate more often? Wha stops you from communicating?

You know you are a watcher when you have

- tracked several months or years of a certain behavior and rehashe the list from time to time,
- kept a list of your partner's transgressions in your head;
- saved up offenses like a coupon card, and when the book is full o stamps, you redeemed it by throwing a fit;
- acted like everything is OK until you reached your limit, and ther morphed into someone with the IQ of a twenty-five-year-old whe acts like a three-year-old.

CRACKLE WITH CREATIVITY

If you or your partner are watchers and counters, then discuss how you might handle your issues in a timely manner. Those with friendship on fir learn to crackle with creativity and face life's challenges together. As Tam Kieves writes, "I've become someone who trusts that though I feel as fragil as a flaming leaf in autumn, I house the capacity for a tidal wave, a meteo shower, white tornado of inspiration." Get in touch with your inner fire o passion, and stop standing and watching on the sidelines.

Don't Let Ghosts Steal Heat

We all bring ghosts from the past into our relationships. Those in loving and lasting unions tame their ghostly ancestors. On a cool Halloween afternoon, Janet and Roger arrived for their therapy session wearing Halloween costumes. They were headed to a Halloween party after their counseling.

GHOST BUSTERS

The costumes prompted me to ask a shadowy yet serious question of the masked and cloaked couple: "What ghosts from the past have haunted your relationship?" After some spirited laughter, Roger answered that he thought his grandfather's boisterous ghost warranted a call to "ghost busters." In my work as a psychotherapist, I have felt like a ghost buster at times because of the invasive influence of ancestors.

INVASIVE ANCESTORS

Roger J. explained how his grandfather's memory haunted Roger's family. "Granddad was a ranting alcoholic." As a child, Roger's mother, Lou, shut down her thinking and feeling and went numb to deal with his tirades. She had no role model because her mother died young, so she grew up in fear as the only child of a tyrannical father. She failed to learn how to make decisions. Although Roger never knew his grandfather, the tyrannical granddad haunted him through his mother's passivity.

Roger was five when his father left; he decided he needed to man up and become the leader. At this young age, he felt better equipped to make decisions than his childlike mom! He felt it was his responsibility to take care of his mother, despite his youth. Roger remembered telling his mother "Now that Dad is no longer here, I'm the man of the house. I will take care of you. No need to worry, Mom."

TAUNTING AND HAUNTING

Janet's mother was bipolar. She dealt with her mother's actions by shutting down and clamming up when her mother unpredictably boiled over. "I learned to tiptoe around the house until her black and scary mood passed over." Each of us is influenced by invisible threats from the past that can wield a lot of undue power over us. We must turn these family "ghosts" into plain old ancestors.

THE UNCONSCIOUS PUZZLE

Their legacies taunted and haunted this couple. At first, it felt comfy and familiar for Roger to make the decisions and dominate the house. Since Janet was used to cowering in the corner, their pattern felt like home. Although Roger hated feeling so overly responsible, it was all he knew. Like pieces of an unconscious puzzle, their behaviors fit together. He took charge. She clammed up.

Over time, Janet felt the need to speak out and accused Roger of running roughshod over her like her mother had done. Roger became defensive and more overbearing. She tried unsuccessfully to hold in her feelings. Their ghosts had risen up to interfere in their relationship. They had to struggle to begin to reclaim their lives from their ancestors. They became ghost busters.

MAKE IT DANCE

When Janet and Roger were able to discuss their ghosts and return them to the past for good, they were able to change the dominant-docile drama. Roger backed off, and Janet stepped up. Framed photos of Granddad and both mothers rest on the mantle as reminders not to replay painful dramas. The ghosts still sneak in at times, but this couple has learned how to deal with them. "If you cannot get rid of the family skeleton, you may as well make it dance" (George Bernard Shaw). Those with friendship on fire tame the inept ghosts of the past and are able to detach from old dramas. They learn to change the channel in their minds so they do not feel like they are watching reruns of *The Addams Family*.

NEW MOVES

My husband and I love to watch a television show called *Dancing with the Stars* because we see stars paired with professional dancers who teach them new patterns of movement. It is amazing to see how the stars progress. We saw race-car driver transform into a ballroom dancer by the end of a season!

Do not take dancing lessons from family ghosts unless they were relationship virtuosos. Find experts to teach you the correct way to dance to maintain friendship on fire. Then *you* can lead the skeletons around the room or, like Janet and Roger, retire their family ghosts to the mantle and learn new dance steps together.

Your Turn

Identify one or more ghosts that hang over your head. What can you do to begin to name and frame your ancestors, understand the legacy, and handle the haunting?

You will need to develop a process to change your behavior because your brain has a built-in protection system that always *intends* to protect you. These behaviors are strong because they help you survive fearful dramas of your youth. You need to reassure your brain that you are now capable of a do-it-yourself dance based upon your present circumstances. You no longer need to be haunted by your past. Build a table to identify and learn to deal with those ghosts.

Roger and Janet's exercise example of their ghostly past:

Spook or Ghost	Ancestral Dance	New Moves
Roger's grandfather	Roger dominates Janet.	Roger listens and shares leadership with Janet.
Janet's mother	Janet tiptoes around in fear.	Janet shows up and speaks up.

Fire Drills

Marsha felt invisible in her family. She was the youngest of three sisters, and her parents were disappointed that she was not a boy. Her older sister was beautiful, and her middle sister was an outstanding scholar. Although Marsha was quite attractive and smart, she perceived that her family was indifferent to her feelings. When she met and married Jeffrey, she felt that she finally had value as a person.

JUST GET OVER IT

Jeffrey was an attorney and thought in a very logical, non-emotional way; Marsha was not comfortable with such a rational approach to life. The result: the relationship became a train wreck. Whenever Marsha felt misunderstood and tried to express her emotions, Jeffrey responded with cool reason. She wondered if he had a pulse.

She felt discounted and invisible. She began to think Jeffrey was just another person who took her for granted and didn't understand her. When she perceived he was unresponsive to her feelings, it reopened deep wounds. The most painful incident was when Marsha was crushed by the behaviors of a mutual friend. Jeffrey responded, "Just get over it."

SEEMINGLY INDIFFERENT REMARKS

When I saw this couple together, it was clear that Jeffrey was devoted to Marsha. I helped Jeffrey understand the history of Marsha's feelings. After hearing the explanation, he realized how seemingly indifferent responses triggered a replay of her past. With better understanding, Marsha and Jeffrey were able to address the differences in how they dealt with their feelings. They agreed that when Marsha felt the old feelings come back, she would not attack her husband with, "You take me for granted," or "You don't understand me." Jeffrey agreed to take time to listen to her emotions and validate her feelings. They were on their way to developing their *friendship on fire*.

A STICK IS A SNAKE

Neuroscientist Joseph LeDoux explains that memories associated with pain and fear cause strong reactions in primitive parts of the brain. Unable to sort out the danger with reason the natural instinct is to fight, freeze, or flee. For example if you were walking in the woods, heard a rattling sound and saw a stick, you probably freaked before you could formulate the word "snake." Your heart raced; your hands sweated. Your response to a perceived, dangerous situation had survival value; it's better to think a stick is a snake than a snake is a stick. A wise African American proverb pays homage to this fact: "He who has been stung by a serpent fears a rope on the ground."

SURVIVAL STUFF

Survival systems in the brain can backfire in relationships. When Jeffrey meant well and was being rational, Marsha saw a snake based on painful past experiences; she would freeze then fight. It is often a huge relief to realize you overread danger in a relationship. There is no need to blame or dwell on the past. Realize your brain in trying to protect you based on past hurts; you see a snake when it is actually a rope.

BENEFIT OF THE DOUBT

In a *friendship on fire,* one gives the other the benefit of the doubt and recognizes the past. With a practice of mindfulness, you calm your brain before you engage your mouth and label your partner a snake.

Love is a practice, a daily choice. Because of past conditioning, many people have trouble sustaining a *friendship on fire.* They may not know that they habitually hijack their own happiness with behaviors learned from their families.

One of the most important functions of *friendship on fire* is to help you identify your conditioned fears so that you can live life more fully. To do so, you need to be open to the pain that is inevitable when a couple is open to mutual acceptance.

HEALING ONE ANOTHER

Couples generally experience only a few kinds of train wrecks that caused their past arguments. If both people look for the underlying meaning of repeated arguments, this will often take them back to the time when they learned defective programming. Intimate partners have the power to help heal one another in a way that no one else can because they replicate the sense of family and bring out the issues of belonging.

Your Turn

Write down three negative belief systems that you learned in your family. For example, "Marriage is about endurance."

Think about your reactions, and ask yourself why they are so strong. Write down ways you can redecide these things in the present. For example, "I will commit to having a healthy and loving marriage."

Think about the way your body reacts if a negative belief system is activated in your relationship. For example, if you believe that marriage is about endurance, do you feel numb at family functions?

How can you begin to pay attention to numb feelings? sad feelings? angry feelings? joyful feelings? As a graduate student in the '70s, I first began this practice and was so numb I had to ask myself, "I wonder what I might be feeling?" Start where you are.

Charlotte Joko Beck observes that when we bring our awareness into the present and experience our feelings, it is like a flame that can burn through egocentric confusion.

Ask yourself how much of the strong reaction comes from old experience.

What decisions did you make about yourself based upon messages you received from your family? from school? from peers?

Who inspired you as a child (you may have been inspired by a fantasy character like Cinderella or Superman)? How do these models of behavior positively affect you? How do they limit you? I have seen countless clients who identified with fantasy characters. For example, I worked with an extremely bright scientist who identified with Snow White. Although she was very successful at work in the lab, in her personal life, she was quite passive as she waited for the perfect prince to kiss her and wake her up to live happily ever after. Sound preposterous? Believe me, there are loads of very smart and capable people who formed an image of themselves from cartoons.

When you have a strong reaction in your relationship, can you ask yourself how much of your reaction may be based on past learning?

How can you and your partner help one another identify and replace old reactions that backfire with healthy solutions?

How can you use the mindfulness practice in this book to help you become calm, centered, and better able to find new solutions?

Keep Sizzle Alive

Sarah and Norman began an exciting courtship as medical interns in a metropolitan emergency room. They met saving the life of a young child. Heady stuff! At the end of an action-packed internship and whirlwind courtship, they married in Venice, Italy. After a three-week tour of Europe, they returned home to residency and married life.

CAREERISTS

Within months, a relationship with such a fantastic beginning became boring. Why? Sarah and Norman became married singles, bored with their relationship and indifferent to each other. Both devoted all their energy to their careers. As it happened, both had careerist parents who believed that nothing was more important than their work. They found little joy in spending time with each other or their children after working hours, and both were prone to boredom-induced depression intensified by the isolation from each other they maintained.

Sarah and Norman opted to let their relationship degenerate into one as zestless as those of their parents. Partly it was because they lacked models and had been led to believe that their parents' type of nonrelationship was what was to be expected when couples chose success. But mainly, like their parents, they didn't believe that maintaining the chemistry that had fired them in the beginning was a priority.

KEEP THE FIRE BURNING

In the beginning, they were fired by the chemistry between them; however, with no idea of how to maintain their *friendship on fire*, they reverted to familiar patterns.

So how do you keep the firing going after the initial high? Don't wait for your partner to make that happen. This turns into a game of "who's on first" as each partner waits for the other to make him/her happy.

Recall things that you did in the beginning of your relationship—stolen kisses, hugs for no reason, spontaneous sex, or belly laughs from shared humor. Don't wait for some structured activity to find joy in every day. It's never too late to begin to learn to love yourself, your partner, and your life.

Behaviors are learned by visual clues, words, and deeds. Picture how you want to approach love and life. Embrace the now.

When Sarah and Norman stopped stealing kisses in the stockroom and whispering compliments in bed at night, their feelings waned. Couples can become lazy about initiating positive behaviors that make them happy. Why? Life changes; other things become a priority or take up so much time that you feel there is little time left for fun. At the end of the day, you may value busyness over love.

You can connect in a matter of seconds repeated through the day—a hug, a wink, high fives, shared humor fuel *friendship on fire*. Over time, people focus on the bad things and discount the good. Rejoice and be grateful for whatever you have. Savor joyful moments, and put away what has been troubling you for a time.

REKINDLE FRIENDSHIP ON FIRE

By their first anniversary, Sarah and Norman realized that their home was Dullsville. They declared their intention to become more affectionate with one another at home, took a cooking class, and decided to move to Israel to fulfill a life purpose when they finished their residencies at the hospital. Together, they rekindled *friendship on fire*.

Your Turn

Ask yourself: Do I love life? As a couple, ask: Do we maintain a *friendship on fire*? If not, why not?

Draw three columns on a blank sheet of paper. List the things that stand in the way of having a *friendship on fire* in the first column. Is this a learned behavior from your family, or is it something else? Write down how you think you got into this rut. In the second, list the things that you are going to do to get out of the rut and create a *friendship on fire* in the third column.

List three joyful activities that you shared at the beginning of your relationship. Discuss whether you want to initiate these behaviors again. If yes, make a commitment to restart them. You can recharge your relationship and get those embers sparking again.

Remember, your spark of awareness is your center. You are free to choose how you will respond to any situation, and you can make a difference every day. Spend some time thinking about how to make your partner happy and enjoy life more together each day. This will only take a few minutes, but can make a lifetime of difference.

What are our barriers?	How did we create the barriers?	How do we return to our *friendship on fire*?
Parents model	Fell into Dullsville habits.	Recommit to loving behaviors.
Demands of Work	Stopped making time for us	Share a common purpose.
Apathy	Stopped being playful and affectionate	Resume our *friendship on fire*.

We waste time looking for the perfect lover, instead of creating the perfect love.

(Tim Robbins)

Pass the Flame to Your Partner

My husband's dream was to retire to the beach. Although that was not my first choice, it was extremely gratifying to see how happy he was when we moved to an oceanfront condo in Florida. How does Robert reciprocate? He is supporting my dreams of writing and traveling to do workshops, which takes him away from his interests.

TWO GIVERS

Faith is believing before receiving.

—Alfred A. Montapert

As I write this section, Robert is supporting me by driving me to a speaking engagement. He was not able to continue working on his medical research for three days, but was willing to forgo this so that I could make my engagement. Friendship on fire requires two givers.

Couples who maintain a *friendship on fire* know it is important to honor their partner's dreams and aspirations to enable them to remain fulfilled and happy. With *friendship on fire* you become a recipient of returned love, support, and affection.

GIFT LOVE

I have found that I love living at the beach and am very touched by my husband's support of my commitment to teach others how to be more loving. It is true that, in giving, we often receive as much or more than we give.

Unfortunately, too often givers marry takers. Such a match cannot become a *friendship on fire* because it is one-sided.

> Need-love says of a woman, "I cannot live without her";
> Gift-love longs to give her happiness, comfort, protection.
> (C. S. Lewis)

Those with *friendship on fire* share the gift of love. They give each other because they are delighted to see each other truly happy and are rewarded with pleasure as they give. Happiness, not a sterile sense of duty, moves them. "The living power of loving kindness—it glows, it shines, it blazes forth" (Buddha).

MIRROR NEURONS

Your brain has the specialized neurons—mirror neurons—that allow you to walk in your partner's shoes; you feel your partner's pain. For example, if you cut your hand, motor cells resonate in your partner's brain so that he shares some of the same feeling.

GIVER-TAKER

The more you use these neurons, the stronger they become. In giver-taker duos, motor neurons become stronger with the giver since in the brain practice makes permanent. On the other hand, takers do not exercise these units, so they do not learn to connect. Last night, we watched a talk show with guests who were obviously a giver-taker duo. She worked three jobs, took care of three children, and looked exhausted. He sometimes worked on weekends and looked perky.

I have learned over the years that it backfires to do things for your partner that he should or must do for himself. The giver on television was enabling her husband to remain a taker while she looked overwhelmed and resentful.

Compassion helps activate happiness centers. Takers miss their recommended daily connection allowance. This is why programs like Alcoholics Anonymous stress the importance of making amends with those they have hurt and making connections with others who suffer in order they are exhibiting their compassion and, in so doing, exercise their mirror neurons..

ENABLING TAKERS

If they are not careful, givers help takers stay stuck in immature, impulsive behaviors and impede the development of emotional growth. If you are in a giver-taker union, remember the lesson taught by Jesus who was egalitarian when he said, "Love one another *as* thyself." This does not mean *instead* of thyself.

Maintaining a *friendship on fire*, you need two givers. The rewards of happiness are a byproduct of the winning formula of two givers on fire. Moreover, the joy of their generous personalities spreads to the world around them.

Your Turn

If you are working as a couple on this exercise, each of you should write down what things you are passionate about. Next, write down what you do to support your partner that makes him or her feel alive and happy. Talk about your passions, and discuss how you help one another realize those dreams.

If you discover a disconnection, this exercise will allow you to work on some things together for the future realization of your dreams.

Here's our sample:

	Passions	Support
Robert	Living at the beach	Move to the beach.
	Mathematics	Find books, listen.
Linda	Writing	Buy her a laptop.
	Teaching	Support her travel.

FIRE OF SAFETY

And at home by the fire, whenever you look up, there shall I be—and whenever I look up, there will be you.

—Thomas Hardy

Introduction
To Fire Of Safety

When someone deeply listens to you
It is like holding out a dented cup
You've had since childhood
And watching it fill up with cold, fresh water.

—John Fox

The "Fire of Safety" section focuses on keeping your connection out of harm's way. When Isaac and Lee first got together, they listened to one another for hours. They were ecstatic to discover friendship on fire and found a safe oasis in life. Both had lived with alcoholic parents and thirsted for attention and genuine affection.

Because this couple did not know how to maintain safety in a relationship, they began to attack one another. Fortunately, they came for counseling when things got out of hand and learned ways to safeguard against their vulnerabilities.

Together, we identified the ways that they assailed the other when threatened. They learned to tell the truth with love and listen with compassion. It took lots of practice for them to refrain from striking out at one another and take the time to formulate constructive assertions. Most important, they learned to forgive themselves and one another as well as to convert the negative energy to good deeds.

The "Fire of Safety" section helps you

➤ manage the heat in your relationship through controlled burns,
➤ provide a safety net for one another,
➤ remove yourself if you are burned by your partner's flame instead of remaining and complaining,
➤ regulate the thermostat of your relationship so you can cool down or heat up,
➤ avoid arguments when there is drinking (too much alcohol can flambé your connection),
➤ accept one another as is,
➤ remember all the magnificent moments of attraction and forgive your partner's faults,
➤ avoid holding on to anger,
➤ kindle one another's spirit,
➤ tell the truth with love, and
➤ listen with compassion.

Depression Can Dampen the Fire

The last and most important frontier is the human mind. It is knowing ourselves, and most importantly, from the inside. The last frontier is our own consciousness.

—Jon Kabat-Zinn

Barbara was a lovely and outgoing woman of forty, but she had a tendency to harbor negative thoughts about herself and others. She was often critical of her husband and children, judging them harshly and not readily forgiving what she perceived to be failures. She was equally unforgiving with herself.

EXISTING WITHOUT LIVING

When Barbara came in for therapy, she was a person without joy, bored and weary of life. Burdened by gloom and pessimism, she existed without really living. Recovery is not a high-speed race; it takes time. Barbara came to realize that her attitudes and values had been shaped largely by the family in which she grew up. Her parents tended to view the world, and each other, in a negative light. Their habit of criticizing their children and each other made family life practically unbearable.

VERBAL JUNK FOOD

Just as you need to watch what you eat in order to maintain a healthy body, you need to watch what you think in order to maintain a healthy mind. Part of Barbara's healing was a mindfulness practice to increase thoughts of acceptance of herself and others. Like changing your food diet, it takes time and practice to change thought choices.

Barbara began a regular practice of mindfulness to watch out for the junk food words and thoughts she was putting in her mind and practice healthier choices. This practice comforted her and allowed her to focus on positive qualities and endeavor to understand weaknesses without condemning those closest to her. Knowing how destructive guilt can be, how her own guilt generated depression, she refrained from making others feel guilty by criticizing their faults. She let her thoughts and actions be informed by understanding, compassion, and love.

As a result, Barbara and her family came to understand how her guilt and a sense of inadequacy had begotten a judgmental attitude toward them. As she jettisoned verbal junk food, she was able to increase her appreciation for her husband and each of her children as individuals and experience the warmth of a close relationship in the present moment. Depression is a complex, potentially dangerous condition, but it is treatable. Someone who is deeply depressed or possibly bipolar needs a psychiatric evaluation diagnosis, and prescribed medical treatment.

The less severe case of Barbara's depression not only illustrates how depression can extinguish the flames that warm a relationship, but also how, with therapy and possibly medication, those flames can be brought back to life.

Your Turn

If you experienced a negative family life, think about the thought habits that you may have developed over the years and what you can do to change your thinking.

Answer the following questions, which may help you to realize depression may be a problem for you.

- Do I tend to be in a bad mood most of the time?
- Do I often feel like I have nothing to look forward to?

- Do I tend to think negatively about myself much of the time?
- Do I often think of my family members and friends in a critical way?
- Do I often think that I am an inadequate or bad person?
- Do I isolate myself and perhaps drink too much, eat too much, or lose myself in solitary activities, like television or computer activities to avoid painful thinking?
- Am I tired too much of the time?
- Do I find myself having trouble going to sleep or having early morning awakenings?
- Do I have trouble enjoying daily activities?
- Am I unable to remember when I felt happy?
- Do I have thoughts of suicide?
- Have I gained or lost more that ten pounds within the last six months?

If you answered yes to most of these questions, you can talk to your family doctor about treatment for depression. Depression is very treatable, and your doctor can assist you in finding the right kind of help. You can also ask the doctor's office for a psychotherapy referral.

Acceptance Fuels Security

I was burned out from exhaustion, buried in the hail, poisoned in the bushes, blown out on the trail; hunted like a crocodile, ravaged in the corn, "Com in," she said, "I'll give ya shelter from the storm.
—Bob Dylan

When Lindsey was approaching a commitment to her husband, Rob, she decided she wanted to be sure he was aware of her faults. She called him and asked to meet for dinner. She was a wreck as she began to write a list of all her faults to present to him over dinner. She was convinced that he would dump her after reading the list, but she knew she had to face these issues.

When Rob read the list, he looked over the dinner table and smiled. "I already know this stuff. I want *you*."

In a *friendship on fire*, you are the real you with a partner who keeps your secrets. Couples in fun and loving relationships know shocking things about their humanness the way one snores, acts grouchy, loses stuff, and is loved anyway! Billy Joel expressed this well in his song, "I love you just the way you are."

Those with *friendship on fire* are loyal keepers of secrets. Betraying each other's privacy is unthinkable and taboo in loving unions.

SEND HEALING THROUGH YOUR HEART

A helpful practice when you feel stuck in judgment of self or others is to imagine the beautiful, warm golden light that is raining down on you from God. Imagine that loving and healing light can be absorbed into your heart. Absorb that healing warmth into your own heart, and then allow it to flow through you and out to another person. In this way, you can sit and absorb healing, and then send that out to your partner. I have found this to be very powerful if my husband and I are in a conflict. Numerous times, this practice has moved and healed us without words. As I sit in one room and absorb and send the light, it positively affects both of us!

ACCEPT LIFE

The ability to let go and accept life unfolds over time. As you become more open and less judgmental of yourself and others, new challenges will become less daunting, and you will operate more from love and less from fear. Do not become discouraged as you practice new ways of thinking and behaving. As you master inner and outer learning, you will one day be living wholeheartedly the present moment.

Your Turn

Answer the following questions:

- Do you accept your partner's flaws? (This does not mean you have to *like* those traits.)
- Does your partner accept your shortcomings?
- Will you protect shared secrets of personal and physical flaws?
- Are you each willing to protect the vulnerability of your partner?
- Do you agree to avoid using faults as ammunition against each other?
- Will you support one another to become better people?
- Are you willing to help your partner if they want to change?
- Do you agree to avoid put-downs?

ACCEPTANCE

Make a list of your flaws as Lindsey did. First, make sure you can accept these things about yourself. If you have trouble with self-acceptance, do the mindfulness practice.

Here are some examples. Start your sentences with "I accept myself for

- being disorganized.
- running late.
- talking too fast.

This sounds like a strange approach, but it helps you like and accept yourself the way you are. Acceptance leads the way toward solutions. This is the reason every speaker at an AA meeting begins with "I am an alcoholic." This is the first step toward change. The irony is that when you are gentle, good-humored, and accepting of your shortcomings, it is much easier to change. When you are overly self-critical, you may want to hide your faults, assuming that you can't change.

This practice will help you like yourself and give you more strength to change if that is what you want.

- As a couple, discuss ways to make it safe to have faults without feeling as if you are being criticized. Your partner might complain about your need to save every slip of paper, but he or she will refrain from calling you a pack rat. Calling someone a "pack rat" is name-calling and off limits unless said with humor and acceptance.
- Name three ways to make each of you feel freer about yourself and your partner.

If your partner tells others secrets about you that embarrass you or calls you names, check out the "I don't go for that" section of the book where we define abusive behaviors.

- Great wisdom from the Bible inspires us to "love one another as yourself." Have you changed it in your mind to love one another instead of yourself? If so, how does this belief affect your life? How can you love others and yourself?
- Do you (or your partner) know how to take care of yourself yet have trouble with a practice of love for the other?
- How can you get a better balance between love of self and one another?

Create a Peaceful Glow

Though we travel the world over to find the beautiful, we must carry it with us or we will not find it.

—Ralph Waldo Emerson

At the end of Jan's workday, she needed to unwind and regain her peace of mind; running did it for her. However, Tom needed his mopey-mood time when he arrived home from work. Being around Tom during his unwinding time was a downer, a negative and draining experience for Jan, so she developed after-work personal time for both of them. While Jan ran, Tom snapped out of the mopes.

CHILL TREATMENT

Moods are contagious so couples with a *friendship on fire* learn ways to calm themselves down instead of berating or placating their partner. You can use relaxation CDs, music, or a centering prayer to calm you down and prevent negative chemicals from spreading around the house. You have a choice. Don't get sucked into the vacuum cleaner of negative moods; your energy drive will disappear. Learn how to live within yourself.

Your Turn

A helpful and simple strategy to calm and invite inner peace is to focus on your breath. As you breathe in, think the word "be" and as you breathe out, think the word "calm." If other thoughts enter your mind, that is OK—just refocus on the breath and the words "be calm." Breathe deeply down to your diaphragm—deep calming, healing breath—you can think in the calming breath as a way of breathing in God. You can shift from "be calm" to imagining that you breathe in God's golden healing light and breathe out painful emotions like fear and rage. The negative emotions dissolve in the golden healing light.

Consider the following questions:

- Are you able to sit still and calm yourself?
- How can you use a centering practice to help you become a better person? A better partner?
- How is the balance in your relationship between closeness and solitude? Do you have too much of either?
- How well can you detach yourself from destructive interactions?
- How might you use a centering practice to detach from the destructive and open up to grace and peace?
- In what other ways do you get centered and peaceful? What other strategies can you use to detach from destructive thoughts and interactions?
- How does your body react when you have a chance to get centered?
- How can you listen to your body to know when to detach and practice centering?
- How much time can you commit to awareness practice during the day (recommended: three times a day in five-minute segments upon awakening, during the day, when you are ready to go to sleep)?

Burn Away Adversity

You can be mentally and physically healthier, wealthier, and probably skinnier by maintaining a *friendship on fire*. Couples with loving and lasting unions look out for each other's health. If both are working, they are mutually supportive and view their combined income as a joint product of their devotion to their relationship. If only one partner is working, the contribution of the other as a supportive homemaker is equally valued.

Margaret and Ian are still active in their eighties. They celebrated their sixtieth wedding anniversary with their three adult children and eight grandchildren by returning to New York City where they spent their honeymoon. Since they are in good health, they were able to take everyone on a tour and laugh about the clueless young couple that stood in these same places over a half century earlier.

Margaret and Ian share a history that includes the good, the bad, and the ugly. Ian served in the South Pacific in the Second World War. His son was two years old before he held him. Ian and Margaret faced economic and emotional hardships, including the loss of a three-month-old baby, the loss of Margaret's sister to cancer in her forties, and her mother to Alzheimer's disease.

ENDURING LOVE

You cannot maintain a lasting *friendship on fire* without some pain. Adversity paves the path to wholeness. Pain shared with passion helps a couple learn to cope emotionally and become mentors for others. Margaret and Ian are experts at controlled burns. Resentments are burdens that they refuse to carry. Their ability to forgive and burn off bad feelings allows them to sustain joy, abundance, and mutual giving.

Ian and Margaret's enduring love is an inspiration to the younger generations. Since love and joy are contagious, they are the center of family celebrations. Their *friendship on fire* transforms difficulties into love.

Your Turn

Using Ian and Margaret as a model, talk about how you might repair conflicts with controlled burns.

Write positive and realistic goals for celebration and sharing. Describe them so that you will know when you or you and your partner have accomplished your goals. For example, let's look at what Ian and Margaret did when they set their goals early in their marriage:

- We will share our love of the outdoors through regular walks and camping trips.
- When we have children, we will make sure that we set aside alone time for us to be together.
- When we disagree about the children, we will talk out our differences when we are alone and not in front of the kids.
- We will share a spiritual practice.
- We will encourage one another to keep our individual interests.
- We will share the leadership in the family according to our strengths and ability.
- We will maintain a sense of humor.
- We will repair our relationship after arguments.

These goals continue to serve them well.

Whatever your goals, it will take commitment, practice, and support of one another to attain them.

Tending the Coals

Frank and Nola had been a couple for two years. In the beginning, they fell over each other making one another happy; there was fire in the relationship. After dating about six months, Nola began to give Frank the cold shoulder when he was late picking her up. He countered by not calling for several days. Instead of trading fun and loving behaviors, they began to trade negative behaviors. The fire went out, and there were no embers to rekindle the flame.

FEELINGS FOLLOW BEHAVIOR

Since feelings follow behavior, Frank and Nola were often unhappy when they were together. The negative exchanges replaced the fun and loving feelings with downers. Unfortunately, the toxic relationship ended badly. The gamey quality of their fearful and aggressive interactions kept them self-absorbed, and they lost their connection.

"WHAT YOU ARE LOOKING FOR IS WHO IS LOOKING"

After a nasty breakup, an angry Nola sat on my couch berating Frank. I gently interrupted her with, "So you are telling me you wanted a lasting and loving union and you worked as hard as possible to push him away." After a few moments of going ballistic, Nola had the hint of a smile on her face, "Yeah, I guess I did act like a big B, huh?" In this moment of self-recognition, Nola began to free herself from destructive actions and break out of the prison of old conditioning. As St. Francis observed, "What you are looking for is who is looking."

YOUR BRAIN IS WIRED FOR LOVE

When you are compassionate and giving, your brain generates positive chemicals. When you are excited about a surprise for your partner, there is a sense of exhilaration. The positive chemicals generated by helping others counteract the negative chemicals from anger, despair, and depression. Some of these chemicals, called neurotransmitters, can alter bodily functions such as eating, sleeping, and sexual activity as well as negative thoughts and moods. On the other hand, endorphins can make you feel really good and give you a runner's high. Your brain is wired for love. When you express love in the here and now, your body glows, but negative reactions scorch with toxic chemicals.

Years ago, my daughter-in-law, Jennifer, found herself in a catch-22 when she and my stepson, Blake, moved to California. She was a graduate nurse who needed to get experience, but she was not able to get experience because she had not worked as an RN. Jennifer called her mother, a very wise woman, and expressed despair about not finding a job.

Her mother remembered that Jennifer had often expressed a desire to work with cancer patients and told her, "Jennifer, get out of the house and go volunteer for cancer patients." As a result of her volunteer work at the cancer center, Jennifer was able to get a job. In the meantime, her mood was considerably elevated by doing meaningful work that touched her heart.

Jennifer has continued working with cancer patients for a number of years and still gains satisfaction from helping others. Her positive emotions show in how she relates to her husband and her children.

BRAIN TRAIN

Think of your brain pathways as a train with a series of branch tracks. Remember all those movies where guys jump from car to car on top of the train? Sometimes, change feels like that since your brain believes that the familiar keeps you safe even though the familiar may no longer be good for you.

Many people learned to be self-centered to survive in hostile families or environments. For example, if you were picked on by older siblings you may have learned to cut your losses by keeping your distance from others. If you want a *friendship on fire*, you may need to jump on a train headed in a different direction. Remind yourself to choose the route of love instead of fear.

THE BRAIN RETURNS TO FAMILIAR ROUTES

The brain returns to the familiar when you are stressed or not sure of the way to go. Through a practice of mindfulness, you gain awareness of destructive habits. By looking without judgment, you watch your brain steam ahead in the wrong direction. You can retrain your brain to head in the direction of love and wholeness. As Jon Kabat-Zinn cautions that even though our thoughts are insubstantial and evanescent, "they are so seductive." The train is out of the station before you know it, steaming in a destructive direction.

TO GIVE IS TO RECEIVE

Those in loving and lasting relationships have learned that to give is to receive. They are good at keeping their positive chemicals flowing by giving and receiving, not material things but looks, smiles, or words of fondness or encouragement. "To love and be loved" is the motto of *friendship on fire*.

If you are in a rut, remember that to overcome negative emotions, you need to develop more powerful positive emotions. In the brain, *practice makes permanent*. Self-centeredness can destroy inner peace. You can change your thought patterns through repetition: *practice, practice, practice*.

WHO ARE YOU REALLY?

For Nola, it was so seductive to say mean and hateful things because she was easily threatened. In one session, I observed that although she was very spiritual and believed with all her heart that Higher Power accompanied her, she sure felt small and cornered a lot. This time, she laughed, "Yea, I act a lot like my Chihuahua . . . I attack because I feel so small and helpless." I asked her how big she felt spiritually, and she answered that she could handle anything. "So why do you need to attack so much?" From the perspective of her higher self, Nola learned to stop in her tracks and remind herself who she really was.

Your Turn

- Identify ways to figure out if you may be stuck on a pity-party track.
- Identify ways you can reach out to help others.
  * You can take the signature values test online for free at *www. authentichappiness.com*. See if you are living according to your deepest values.
- When you are stuck or fear taking risks, ask yourself how this fear protected you in the past (e.g., in the past, your home may have been filled with strife so you fear commitment).
- Reaffirm your decision to make choices that are good for you.
- Prepare for the fearful emotions that arise to protect you when you face change.
- Pick up your fear, stare it in the face, and risk new behaviors that you know are in your best interest (e.g., if you were picked on and are afraid of others, visualize yourself as calm and relaxed around others). Then go out and practice. Since your brain means to protect you, it may be necessary to put yourself back in fearful situation to convince yourself things are different. For example, if you are thrown off a horse, you regain your confidence by riding again. Use the centering practice often, and touch your right wrist when you feel very relaxed. When you are back in a fearful situation, touching your wrist has become a conditioned response reminding you to relax. The more you practice centering and calming yourself, the more natural it becomes.
- I have done a practice of centering and visualization for many years. Recently, I was backing my car out of the garage, and a huge snake was caught in the garage door. I was filled with fear and dread. I backed out as soon as possible and knew I had to pull myself together to drive to an important meeting. I simply reached over and touched my right wrist, and I felt calmed and centered. What a test!
- With practice, your behavior will begin to follow the positive pictures on your mind and repeated affirmations.

Friendship on fire implies two people living passionately and encouraging one another to be all they can be. "Change may wear a wolf suit. Still don't be fooled. It's wild, abundant magic knocking on your door" (Tama Kieves).

Fuel Your Partner's Fire

Fern, thirtysomething, was brimming with humor and energy. When she came for her first therapy session, she was warm, friendly, and assertive. For the next session, Fern came with her fiancé, Gene. She was no longer the friendly, assertive young woman; she had morphed into a docile namby-pamby. There had clearly been a brain drain. She sat like a marble statue barely breathing.

SISTER THE GREAT

What happened? Why was she so inhibited, so withdrawn, when she was with her fiancé? Fern grew up with stern and judgmental parents. Her older sister was Dad's favorite, and Fern was unfavorably compared with this Sister the Great. The comparison led to a lack of self-worth that followed Fern into adult life.

She played out this script of low self-worth with Gene. She thought of Gene as a father figure who never saw the best in her. Deep down, she feared that she would never measure up to what Gene wanted in a wife, so she measured her words in order to appear to gain his approval.

BARGAIN-BASEMENT BRIDE

In Fern's mind, she was a bargain-basement bride so she needed to *act* like a mannequin in a store window. By revealing more of herself in words or deeds, she believed she would be unfavorably compared to others.

Fern thought that if she looked good and said little, she would be more accepted by Gene the Great.

YOUR BRAIN TRIES TO PROTECT YOU

As a child, you made critical decisions based on your perceptions. Your brain stored what you felt, saw, and heard. Later, you projected past perceptions onto your present reality. You still rerun the tape of your past experiences, once seen but never forgotten. Our brain *protects* us; we learn by experience. Fern's protection was silence when she was with her father; maintaining silence was better than providing more material for put-downs.

How did Gene play out his part in this drama? He had learned critical, perfectionist expectations from his family so he would make references to Fern's love handles and give gaga reactions to svelte women they passed on the street. Fern was a beautiful size 4! He too was caught in a fantasy world that kept him from a meaningful life. They were compatible in unhealthy ways. Gene compared Fern to perfection; she compared herself to imperfection.

Once they were aware of their interlocking programming, they began awareness practice, writing about and practicing positive ways to create a change in the direction of their thinking. "True Love always brings joy to ourselves and the one we love. If our love does not bring joy to both of us, it is not true love" (Thich Nhat Hanh).

Very often in relationships, we have difficulty being fun and loving because we are thinking about potential. This is the voice inside that second-guesses things like, "I should have . . ." or "I could have . . ." Fern and Gene needed to become aware of what was, not what should be. Judgment blocks love. This couple was so busy judging one another that there was little time for loving and living.

Your Turn

Whether you are in a relationship or between relationships, think through the following questions, and write down a response to each. Be honest; no one else has to read what you write. By writing it down, you may see what has affected your relationships.

- Do you believe you need a makeover in order to be loved?

- Did you pick your partner because of the potential to change them into someone different from who they are?
- Do you allow judgments of self or others to crowd out love and life?
- When did you first start showing the world a false self and why?
- What do you think it would look like if you acted like the real deal?
- What would the real deal look like to you?

Fern's responses would look like this:

- Yes, I wanted to be someone else that others could be attracted to and admire, but I felt that I rated as an also-ran in my life.
- I didn't pick Gene consciously to change him. I just wanted him to be good to me and not put me down or think of me as second best or an also-ran. I wanted his approval.
- I know I don't act like what I really feel inside, so my actions don't always match what I want to say. I guess I send a lot of mixed messages.
- I learned to take on a different me with my father and sister; it was easier to remain silent than to listen to their critical remarks.
- My real deal is for me to be the best me and be comfortable in my relationships without having to hide my true self.

Heart Burns

We have to face the pain we have been running from. In fact, we need to learn to rest it and let its searing power transform us.
— Charlotte Joko Beck

Bart was a forty-seven-year-old straight-laced and successful businessman with very high blood pressure. After writing a prescription for him, his physician referred him to me for stress management. Although he was happy with his work, he often had pressing deadlines to meet and presentations to give, but his biggest concerns were at home.

SAFETY VALVES

In the last six months, Bart had felt a gnawing sense of dissatisfaction with his homelife. He knew his wife of fifteen years had one affair in the past and feared she was having another.

Bart had no safety valve to release his pent-up feelings. Years of holding in strong feelings had taken a toll on him. His stress hormones were wreaking havoc on his mind and body. What happened to Bart? His fight-or-flight reaction put his system in overdrive and kept his motor racing. This reaction is designed to help you face a sudden need for extra energy. However, people like Bart overuse their brain's alarm system and worry too much with no action. While some stress hormones are helpful and may even save your life, the drip-drip-drip over time with no way to empty the buildup is hazardous to your health.

CHEMICAL PIT CREW

The gunning of Bart's stress engine caused his pit crew of hormone chemicals—namely adrenaline and cortisol—from his adrenal glands to speed up his heart rate, elevate his blood pressure, provide a surge of energy, and shoot up his blood sugar. Bart's health suffered because he did not face his feelings. As Bart spilled the beans about his feelings and dealt directly with his wife, his symptoms improved. He used awareness practice and writing to release his hurt and venomous feelings and felt more at peace. As Bart opened up to his deepest feelings, the grip of his feelings of hurt and rage loosened, allowing his mind and body to be liberated from daily suffering.

Although he decided to get a divorce when he dealt with his wife's second affair, he was able to handle the situation with integrity and get on with his life.

Your Turn

Close your eyes and picture yourself beside a large body of water. Look around your feet and notice small stones. Take a moment to put a stone in your left hand and a stone in your right. Each stone represents a problem you are ready to let go. Turn your attention to the stone in your right hand. What problem does that represent that you are ready to let go of? Then turn your attention to the stone in your right hand. What problem does that represent that you are ready to let go of? Take three deep, cleansing breaths. When you are clear about the problems, throw the first stone in the water to suggest that your brain find ways to let go. Repeat with second stone.

Once you have thrown the stones, take a moment to picture you life without these problems. How would it look different? Picture yourself calm, centered, and at peace, trusting that God can help your mind find unconscious solutions to your problems.

Practice this at least twice a day; picture turning your problem over to a higher power to be solved in the divine order, letting go of problems that do not serve you.

D. H. Lawrence said, "We are cut off from the great sources of our inward nourishment and renewal." Tap into your great unconscious reservoirs by listening to your body to identify problems and then turning them over to God for your perfect solution in the divine order. Learn to trust the wisdom of your body and soul.

Next, think about the health of your parents and family members. What connections do you see between good physical and mental health and positive behaviors toward one another? Identify those habits you might need to change in order to have a healthy and lasting love.

Make four columns on a sheet of paper with the following headings:

1. Family Behavior
2. Health Effect
3. Harm to Health
4. Healthy Behaviors

Then fill in the blanks as each column relates to you.

Here is Bart's example:

Family Behavior	Health Effect	Harm to Health	Healthy Behaviors
Family did not express feelings Distance	Storm of stress	High blood pressure, increased blood sugar Possible heart attack, and diabetes	Express feelings in journal to wife, aerobic exercise Visualize healthy self and seek inner nourishment

Smile Spreads the Glow

If you want to be loved, be lovable.

—Ovid

Thirty years ago, an interesting research study began in California, the study of smiles. Researchers took a yearbook and identified the Duchenne smile in graduating coeds.

A Duchenne smile is one that you cannot fake. Involuntary muscles in your face, including those around your eyes, control your mouth. Your subconscious brain sends signals to your muscles so the information that you are processing—words, sounds, smells, and memories—control your involuntary smile. You smile from the inside out.

A non-Duchenne smile or false smile is controlled by conscious thoughts. It involves only the mouth. This is a camera smile.

Researchers followed the young women who had Duchenne smiles and discovered they were happier and better adjusted thirty years later! It is amazing to imagine that a smile would predict happiness and life adjustment. Researchers found that these coeds had better, more lasting relationships, careers, and better-adjusted children. Never underestimate the power of a smile that begins on the inside.

Friendship on fire requires real smiles. A smile is contagious because it generates positive chemicals, endorphins, within your body. People who have meaningful, lasting relationships know the power of smiles. Smile deliberately; notice the little chemical boost. Brain scans show pleasure centers light up when a smile is the real deal but show no activity when it is a fake. Check out the outer edges of the eyebrows if you want to know if a smile is a real sign of internal happiness; if they do not drop a bit, it is a fake smile.

Negative moods are also contagious. There is the temptation to divert your own foul mood and dump on people closest to you. Negative emotions are like a virus; they spread easily. However, remember you *choose* whether to wear a smile or a frown. Couples who maintain a *friendship on fire* learn to manage their negative moods by taking responsibility and not blaming their partners.

A smile exercises your facial muscles in a positive way, resulting in laugh lines, but a frown adds to your wrinkles. Work on your thought patterns; happiness is an inside job.

An approach that I use with parents is to show them how to help their children learn to have a "best bad day," explained in my book *The Brian Train*. For example, if you are having a terrible day before searching for solutions to the problem, watch a funny movie, listen to your favorite music, or exercise. By holding the bad day at bay with some positive thoughts, you are more likely to come up with a solution.

In South America and the impoverished Caribbean, they say, "No problem." We need to remember that others experience far more hardships than we realize; you need to face your problems without making yourself and others have a bad day. Most people often forget how fortunate they are; they want life to be bad-day free.

We will never know how much just a simple smile will do.
(Mother Teresa)

Your Turn

When you find yourself having a bad day, think about what caused it, and write it down in your journal so that you can keep a record of what puts you into a bad-day syndrome. Identify ways *you* can get into a better mood—music, exercise, journaling, or gardening. Make a note of what helps you. Identify people in your life who are stress producers and avoid them as much as possible.

If you and your partner catch each other's bad moods, identify ways you can stay cheerful even when the other is in a funk. Develop ways to let your partner know when you are having a bad day and need alone time to heal.

> A sign of maturity is when we are able to find joy amid suffering.
> (Joseph Campbell)

Firemen Are Team Players

When dinnertime rolls around, Sarah begins cooking. She knows that Bob can cook, but he doesn't like to, so she prepares the main course; and Bob is responsible for preparing dessert, usually ice cream, because it tastes good and it's easy. After dessert Bob does the dishes, and Sarah spends time reading a book while she waits for Bob to finish.

Sharing everyday tasks is an important aspect of fun and loving relationships. The happiest couples share chores based on what they do best. They share in household tasks to give them more time to spend having fun together. Tasks or chores are best defined by skill and desire and not by gender. Bob does the washing, and Sarah does the ironing. Bob does the banking, and Sarah pays bills on the computer.

The biblical phrase, "Two are better than one because they have good reward for their labor," is evident in a *friendship on fire*. Sharing daily tasks gives both partners more time to pursue their individual pastimes and more time to spend together. Traditional gender roles are history; decide what works best for you. Resentment builds when daily tasks and responsibilities are one-sided; you begin thinking about your partner in a negative way. You perceive that he/she is indifferent to your needs. Communication breaks down and you develop a new mindset with regards to your relationship. Pent-up anger and resentment lead to arguments and accusations of not caring.

Your Turn

Make a list of daily, weekly, monthly, and yearly tasks and check things off as they get done. Don't forget to include household and car maintenance insurance payments, health care visits, and all the mundane things of daily living. Busy lives mean we neglect some of the things we like to do least. The list keeps you on track. Don't forget the fun things; get out that dream list you have stored in the back of your mind. Talk about ways that you can help free one another up through division of labor or saving funds to realize your dreams or hobbies.

Now go back and consider who is best suited for each task on the basis of ability and desire. If you can afford hired help, go for it.

For most people, leadership needs to be shared among family members. If you have children, then include them on a level that is reasonable for their age and ability. Getting them involved at an early age helps them develop motor skills and provides a start toward independence.

Sharing the burdens or dreams brings you closer together.

Layaway Smothers Love

Judy was very shy and felt undesirable because she was teased about her weight as a child. Although she had grown into a successful, svelte, and attractive adult, she still hid out at home. During therapy, she revealed that she wanted a family more than anything. I asked, "Do you plan to accomplish this by barricading yourself at home every night?"

Judy had placed herself on an unspecified layaway. She had no idea when she would be picked up. In her dream, a handsome hunk would show up and take her out. Her life was passing her by as she waited in the back.

Sometimes, I use the Colombo approach—play dumb. This creates a fun environment for feedback. In one of Judy's sessions, I said, "So the most important thing in your life is to find a good relationship, and the way that you go about this is to stay home alone every night. Is that right?" This approach usually brings on a smile. Judy was in danger because she did not take risks.

There is no safety but in risking all for love. (Shakespeare)

If you want to live longer and be happier and healthier, then pick a good partner with whom you can share your life. People who are in stable long-term relationships have more frequent and better sex. They learn each other's buttons and polish the pleasures of sexual play. If you are in a *friendship on fire,* you need to risk new behaviors.

Your Turn

Have you put your lamp under a bushel? Do you say, "I know no one will want me, so I cut my losses and will not go to the party"?

Practice the following exercise, and then write down what you notice.

Focus on your breathing. Count seven deep breaths. Go to your beautiful peaceful place in your mind. Imagine that you are at a railroad station where you board a special train that travels back to the time you began to withdraw. How old were you? Feel compassion for the child who decided that he/she needed this behavior for protection. Let the emotions flow.

Now imagine yourself as an adult. How would you tell this child it is safe to take chances on relationships? It is likely that the child decided she was unworthy or inadequate. As an adult, how would you explain to her that we are all flawed in some way and help her change her decision?

If this exercise brings up pain, recognize that all of us need to work on pain from our pasts. Don't be hard on yourself. Notice where you feel the pain in your body. Do you want to push the pain away? Imagine your body is an open space, and the pain can be there without resistance. See if this opening changes the pain. Allow it to flow into space. Too often, we want to clamp down on pain instead of listening and grieving. Dragging around the past hurts. Learn to give it the heave-ho.

Imagine you can help the child make a new decision and turn it into a positive statement: "I am a loving person, and I deserve to be loved." Say it over and over again. You can do this exercise as many times as you need to until you are able to change your thinking and behavior.

Visualize your life the way you want it to be. Thank your unconscious mind for trying to protect you from pain but let your mind know that you plan to make new pictures to follow, accept, and let go of past decisions and move into future possibilities.

Chill Before Firing

Sandra and John were in their mid thirties with two children. One night, they hired a babysitter and went to a friend's party. Most of the people there were John's coworkers, and he paid little attention to Sandra. She felt hurt and neglected and then started to fume. It added fuel to her fire when John spent an hour in a conversation with a hot blonde coworker.

From Sandra's point of view, it was reasonable to explode at John later that evening when they got in the car to go home. John became extremely defensive and failed to understand why Sandra was so riled.

The next day, John Jr. had a soccer game; both parents went to the game but didn't speak to one another except for the necessary discussion about the kids and the game. Later that night after the children went to bed; Sandra and John sat down together and discussed their differences. Fortunately, both had taken time to calm down and refrained from saying things that they would later regret.

SHIFT OUT OF ATTACK MODE

Sandra was able to shift out of attack mode, and John listened carefully while she explained how she felt at the party. Rather than be on the defensive, John was able to put himself in his wife's shoes and imagined how it felt to stand alone for hours and watch him with his cohorts and the hot-looking blonde.

As a result of the conversation, they followed a formula that worked: *strike when the iron is cold.*

Sandra agreed to work on her temper. They agreed that at future parties, if either felt uncomfortable, they would use a signal as a sign to reconnect if one or the other was feeling neglected.

One of the most important practices in maintaining a *friendship on fire* is the ability to repair after differences. To maintain the practice of love, couples need to learn to connect, disengage, bridge their differences, and reconnect:

1. **Connect:** As you are trying to connect with someone, visualize the other person's life, and how he or she came to be where he or she is today. It's not easy. You tend to use your own set of rules or brain paths to judge others.

    John could begin to relate to Sandra's concerns when he imagined standing in her shoes. Sandra was brought up to be polite and proper in public. Her parents were very reserved. John's parents, on the other hand, were very outgoing. His mother was a charming hostess who tended to be effusive. His father was something of a glad-hander and apt to be flirtatious. Sandra knew them and could see how they had influenced their son.

2. **Disengage:** Find ways to calm yourself—exercise, meditate, write down your thoughts, or walk in the park—until you can change your perspective and begin building a bridge back to your partner. In order to resolve conflict, both people have to lean forward to connect the bridge.

    Sandra takes a slow and mindful walk and breathes deeply to calm down. John slams a basketball around to release tension.

3. **Bridge differences:** This is based upon mutual respect and avoidance of shame and blame or rehashing the past. Your discussion should be based on a present problem. Work as a couple toward finding the best solution. It is very important to work out issues; otherwise, unresolved problems will fester, and walls will build up between you and your partner. Stress cracks develop in the relationship, resulting in a no-win situation. John and Sandra found a solution that worked for both of them.

4. **Reconnect:** After a fight, you need the ability to repair, forgive, live in the present, and restore whatever you have said or done to damage the relationship. Harboring a grudge over an issue and allowing memories of the problem to fester are unhealthy for your mind and body.

Because they followed the necessary steps, John and Sandra cleared the air and were able to enjoy each other again as a loving couple.

Your Turn

If you are not in a relationship, think about past relationships and determine how you handled your connections. Write down the following:

- What part did you play in fighting, and did you fight fairly?
- What did you do to reconnect with your partner?
- What did you do well?
- What can you improve on with your next relationship?

For those of you currently in a relationship, write down the following:

- How well do you connect?
- Do you fight fair?
- How do you reconnect?
- What skills do you need to improve?

Discuss how you can make a better practice of these skills.
Ask one another if you use compassion as you listen.
Here are other questions to answer for yourself, whether in or out of a relationship:

- How do I connect with others?
- Do I fight fair? Or do I fight at all?
- When I fight, what do I do?
- Do I have strategies to calm down before dealing with a conflict?
- Am I able to put myself in others' shoes?
- How well did my family deal with conflict?
- What good strategies did I learn?
- What behaviors bomb when I deal with conflict?
- Am I able to calmly listen to other points of view?
- Am I able to be proactive with solutions instead of reactive?

- Am I able to take a position based on my values in a clear and firm manner?
- How do I reconnect after an argument?
- Do I bear a grudge and harbor resentment?
- Do I bring up past problems and try to make the other person feel bad?
- After we have made up, do I still bring up issues from the past?

Now think about what you need to change, and how you can improve on past behaviors. What do you intend to do and when? Make an agreement with yourself. Write it down; then check it out every few weeks

Ten Ideas For
A Smart Marriage

By, Diane Sollee

1. **Marriage matters.** Married people & their kids do better on *all* measures of health, wealth, happiness, & success. And, married folks report having more & better sex than single or divorced people.
2. **It's not the differences but how we handle them** that separate successful marriages from the failures. Disagreeing doesn't predict divorce. Stonewalling, avoidance, contempt, criticism, and the silent treatment predict divorce. Learn how to disagree in ways that help you fall more in love.
3. **All happily married couples have approximately ten irreconcilable differences**—ten issues they will never resolve. If we switch partners, we just get ten new issues that are likely to be even more annoying and complicated. Sadly, if there are children from an earlier marriage or relationship, disagreements about them go to the top of the list. What's important is to discuss our own set of issues just as we would discuss how to manage living with a chronic bad back or trick knee. We wish they weren't there, but what's important is to keep talking about how to manage them and still do the marriage "dance".
4. **Love is not an absolute** (a yes or no situation) and it's not limited substance. *It's a feeling* and feelings ebb and flow depending on how we treat each other. We can learn new ways to interact and the

feelings "of being in love" can come flowing back, often stronger than before.

5. **Marital satisfaction often dips with the birth of a baby.** That's normal. Marital satisfaction is at its lowest when there are kids in the house between 11 and 16. That's normal. We need to know what to expect, appreciate our parenting partner—and hang in. It makes good sense to stay married for the sake of the kids—and for our own sake. Even with the challenges, it's a lot easier to be a parenting team than to be a single, divorced, or remarried parent. Plus there is a silver lining: satisfaction goes back up with the empty nest. The final stage of marriage—with a job well done—is the real honeymoon period.

6. **Sex ebbs and flows. It comes and goes.** That's normal. Plan for & make time for more "flows".

7. **Creating good marital sex is not about putting the sizzle BACK INTO** your sex life. Early marital sex is sex between strangers—we don't yet know our partner or ourselves. The most passionate sex is intimate sex based on knowing our partner and letting them know us. One of the most important tasks of marriage is to develop a satisfying marital sex style. It's not about going BACK; it's about going FORWARD, together.

8. **Repair attempts are crucial** and are highly predictive of marital happiness. They can be clumsy or funny, even sarcastic, but the willingness to make up after an argument, is central to every happy marriage.

9. **Learn to welcome, embrace and integrate change**—to discuss and update your wishes, hopes & dreams—on a regular basis. We often "interview" each other before marriage and then think "that's it." The marriage vow is a promise to stay married, not to stay the same. (Thank goodness!) Keep up-to-date with changes in your partner. Don't fear changes, celebrate them!

10. **Try several different marriage education courses.** Become informed consumers—rate the courses, discuss what you liked best—which ideas were most helpful. Decide which courses to recommend to your kids, friends and family—which to give as wedding, anniversary and new baby gifts. The courses don't tell you what kind of marriage to have. That's up to you. They give you the tools—the hammers, screwdrivers, and levels—so you can build the kind of marriage that suits you, one which can help you to negotiate, and renegotiate, your own values, meaning, and goals.

Find a class at *http://www.smartmarriages.com/directory_browse.html* Strengthen your own marriage and/or learn how to become a Marriage Educator and teach the courses in your community.

Diane Sollee, founder and director, Smart Marriages

Resources, articles and educational material can be found by going to www. smartmarriages.com

Fighting Breast Cancer
As a Team

by Dr. Linda Miles (reprinted from *Amoena* magazine)

Jan was thirty-four when she was diagnosed with breast cancer. She had two children from a previous marriage and had married a wonderful man, Jeff, less than a year earlier. How could she tell him that she might need a mastectomy when they were still honeymooners?

Her husband's first reaction was to try to fix the problem, "Don't worry, honey, we will get a second opinion."

The second opinion confirmed the diagnosis and recommendation: radical mastectomy with removal of the lymph nodes.

Jeff and Jan became distant, each in his and her own world. Jan felt a deep sense of shame and believed that Jeff would not love her after the surgery; Jeff felt helpless. They cut themselves off from the greatest heater of all: love.

After the initial shock, they turned back toward one another as a couple and looked for professional help. They found a nurse therapist who had been many couples go through treatment and had been inspired by those she had seen triumph in the face of adversity. She helped Jan and Jeff practice the lessons courageous couples had taught her.

She started out by telling them that love is the defiance of despair. She assured them that if they maintained a strong connection through the cancer challenge, they would grow individually and together.

Jan and Jeff decided to redefine the problems they faced as gateways to growth. They decided to avoid attack thoughts as much as possible. They also agreed that peace could be found in the midst of turmoil if they had calm in their hearts. They decided that the decision of whether to have a mastectomy was Jan's. After treatment, she made the decision to exercise regularly and change her diet for health reasons. She joined a spa with a close friend.

Throughout her illness and healing process, Jan worked at noticing the difference between pain and suffering. Pain is a necessary part of life. Suffering is a choice. The pain of breast cancer treatment must be faced in order to heal. On the other hand, Jan realized that she brought on quite a bit of her own suffering by self-attacks. For example, she had thoughts like, "I am defective."

Euripides wrote, "Real friendship is shown in times of trouble." As Jan felt better about herself, she was able to seek support from others. A good friend from her church helped her when she reminded her, "God does not make any junk." As they laughed together, it gave Jan a new perspective on herself; she realized she was hindering her own growth by beating herself up. When those inner attack thoughts started creeping in, she made a conscious effort to replace them with thoughts of gratitude like, "I am grateful for my perfect healing." After a few weeks, she no longer had to work on her positive attitude; it came naturally.

That change in attitude led her toward positive actions like a better diet, regular exercise, and searching for support information on the Internet.

Mother Teresa once said that our best protection is a joyful heart. Jan found that she was drawn to those who could face adversity with a sense of humor like her friend from church. She learned to avoid people who were toxic. Emotions are contagious, and she didn't want to catch bad moods from others.

Although Jan's cancer was serious, it also provided Jan and Jeff an opportunity to deepen their marriage and strengthen their commitment.

How? They learned to banish the half-truths: no more whitewashing a bad day. They learned to be more authentic with one another and to tell the truth with love.

The nurse therapist shared the following ideas with Jan and Jeff to help them learn the secrets of effective communication when handling the life challenge of breast cancer.

1. Forget the Fix-it Approach

By nature, most guys have a common reaction when something is broken: fix it. They replace the broken window, change the flat tire, or get the lawn mower running. Their natural inclination is to stop in and find a way to fix the problem.

There is no easy fix for breast cancer recovery. Jeff had to listen to and learn from Jan and the medical staff before he could help Jan through the recovery. He found out that sometimes, it was something as simple as being there for, and listening to, Jan.

Henri Nouwen wrote, "When we honestly ask ourselves which person in our lives means the most to us, we often find that it is those who, instead of giving much advice, solutions, or cures, have chosen rather to share our pain and touch our wounds with a tender and gentle hand."

Jeff learned to be that tender and gentle hand. Jan also learned to seek out friends who were able to sit with her through the physical and emotional pain. She realized that although people meant well, she actually felt worse after nervous reassurances like, "Get well soon." Jan was already too hard on herself and felt she needed to "just get over it." The acknowledgment that her healing was a process was realistic and encouraging.

2. Accept Reality

Jan learned that love is based on acceptance and not performance. As she learned to accept herself and her cancer, she could open up to the caring of those around her. As long as she was mired in shame and felt bad about herself, she could not see the looks of compassion around her or allow others the opportunity to give from their hearts.

Jan and Jeff needed to work on accepting the situation rather than withdrawing into shame or inadequacy. They learned to talk openly about the cancer and to be gentle with themselves and to one another. They also learned to be open with family and friends, not try to hide behind a false smile.

When she realized that it was up to her to teach others how to treat her, she became more active in letting them know what she needed. Sometimes, she wanted help; and other times, she needed to be left alone.

Jeff realized his role was not that of a protector but that of supporter: he learned to stand behind Jan's decisions during and after the recovery process.

3. Pain Is Unavoidable; Suffering is a Choice

Although life brings pain, internal suffering is often self-imposed.

At first, Jan felt ashamed about her illness; she withdrew from others and suffered in silence. She cut herself off from the healing love of friends and family. She didn't choose to have the pain, but she did choose to suffer alone.

Jan found that it helped her to focus on caring about others. She decided to face her pain, but not give into pity parties. For example, she knew that the nurse who gave her radiation treatments was having a tough pregnancy, so she always asked about her and brought her articles and some things for the baby.

4. Refrain from Lame

Jan and Jeff both learned to avoid lame reassurances. Jeff quit trying to paint a rosy picture by saying things like, "Things are fine, dear," or "I'm sure tomorrow will be a better day." Jan learned to avoid saying she was "just fine" to Jeff when she needed support.

Instead, they told the truth with love and humor. Jan once returned from chemo and told Jeff she hoped that he liked plaid since her chest was marked up that way for radiation.

He laughed and told her, "Why, plaid happens to be my favorite now."

They used humor in defiance of despair.

Many times, friends have no idea of what to say to a woman with breast cancer. Jan learned how to help good friends refrain from the lame by bringing up her condition in an honest and straightforward way when she needed to talk and let them know she did not feel like discussing cancer. She simply told them, "I appreciate your concern, but it would not help me to talk about it right now." She then took the initiative to change the topic to avoid an awkward silence.

5. Don't Reduce a Woman to ABC

In one of her episodes of shame after the mastectomy, Jan exploded at Jeff and told him she would not be measured at an A, B, or C.

Jeff answered her that she was not his A-, B-, or C-cup girl; she was the same Jan that he knew and loved. More importantly, he showed hi love and acceptance through involvement in her treatment, giving her a warm hug for no reason, humor, and lovemaking.

6. Change the Meaning of Sex

Jan and Jeff redefined sex as an exchange of affection and decided they both needed lots of that. They learned to talk openly about hormonal changes like lack of lubrication and a reduction of Jan's sex drive. Some positions were painful for them, so they made some adjustments.

7. Make a Bad Day Better

As a family, they developed a "best bad day" tradition. Jeff started this when Jan was having some bad days during chemo. He helped the children do special things for Jan on those days. One child made place mats, and another one decorated a card. They maintain this tradition to support one another through bad days. It is a powerful model for children to learn compassion and altruism.

8. Enough is Enough

Jan and Jeff taught friends and family when enough is enough. People often say nothing, or they overreact when they learn that their mother, sister, or other relative or friend has breast cancer. Jan knew when enough was enough.

When she was ill, Jeff became the gatekeeper. He encouraged the children to make creative items, initiating the "best bad day" activities for all of them. The children were encouraged to express feelings and fears.

9. Remember the Song in Your Heart

True friends and family know the song in your heart and can sing it back to you when you cannot recall the words. When she was down, Jan's friends and family reminded her of happy memories, the things she had to be thankful for and all the things they had to look forward to when she was better. Every evening, the family told each other things they appreciated to the other thus making positive deposits in the family's emotional bank account.

10. Celebrate Every Day

The biggest lesson Jan and Jeff learned was to be grateful for every day.

It has been eight years since Jan's cancer treatment, but they continue to live in the present as much as possible and share a celebration of life. They go on dates once a week to nurture their connection and romance. They now have a plaque in the kitchen that reads,

> *In the depth of winter I finally learned that*
> *There was within me an invincible summer*

—Camus

Although there were tough times for this family after the breast cancer diagnosis, there were also many gifts and lessons they would use to make their lives better. Although a breast cancer diagnosis presents great challenges, it is an opportunity for us to learn to be more loving.

By using these ten keys, you have the opportunity to heal not only from breast cancer but also from relationships.

Your Turn

Millions of mothers, wives, sisters, daughters, and friends are diagnosed with breast cancer each year;

Review the principles listed in the article, and discuss how you might use these to communicate effectively during this tough time. These principles can also be applied to other forms of cancer or major illness. Fight the cancer and not one another.

www.amoena.com has resources and articles for women with breast cancer and their families.

Alcohol Can Flambé Your Connection

by Kay Dougherty

Melinda met Jack at happy hour at her office and loved his charm and sense of humor. She did not notice that he ordered six drinks that night, or that on their first date, he drank eight beers during a day of sailing.

RED FLAGS

Like many alcoholics, Jack had a high tolerance, and he was smart, affectionate, and funny. Melinda fell head over heels for him.

Their wedding on the beach was a blast and again Melinda missed the red flags. Although she noticed how much he had to drink, Jack laughed, "Honey, this is our wedding. I am celebrating the happiest day of my life."

After the marriage, Melinda continued to deny that Jack had a drinking problem; and he had a million and one excuses for why he had problems keeping a job, missed important meetings, or maxed out the credit cards.

Alcohol and other drug use can significantly affect a relationship. It may be years before a spouse of a substance user believes it is the drug causing the problem.

There is a progression that occurs with the user that is modeled by the family. As abuse/dependency occurs, the user will deny to himself/herself that the alcohol or other drug is the problem—it's the job, the spouse, the kids, etc. The family members, particularly the spouse, will believe these excuses because the alcoholic/addict has "facts" to present (e.g., my boss is on my case, you are never home, the kids are out of control, etc.)

As the addiction gets worse, the addict will attempt to hide the chemical and the problems. (The chemical has become *very important*.) The spouse, or other family member, knows at some level, that if the chemical wasn't there, things would be better, so they search and throw away what they find. This doesn't eliminate the problem; in fact, it only worsens it in the long run.

The addict will begin having work, financial, and legal problems; and the spouse most often will "protect" the user: clean up the vomit, awake the user, drive them to work if a license is suspended, pay the fines, and take over home responsibilities.

Throughout this family progression, the user reinforces that the problem is not the chemical, it is something else. The spouse and other family members feel disoriented and "crazy."

Your Turn

If you are feeling angry, helpless, hopeless, or a martyr, please look at the possibility that alcohol or another drug problem may be the issue. Does your spouse

- Become angry if you mention the use of alcohol or other drugs?
- Spend money budgeted to other things on alcohol etc.?
- Make sure that every activity will have alcohol/drugs present?
- Blame you or others for every problem that occurs?

If this sounds like your family, there *are* things that you can do:

1. Get help for yourself. Go to an Al-Anon or Nar-Anon meeting. These self-help groups are provided especially for the spouse o an alcohol or drug abuser. You will meet other individuals who ar or have been where you are. Try more than one if you don't fee comfortable with the first. Al-Anon and Nar-Anon can help yo

set the boundaries you need so that your spouse begins to receive the consequences of his/her use.

2. Find a competent substance-abuse professional. (You can search the phone directory under "chemical dependency," "drug treatment," or "psychologists," "social workers," "mental health professionals," *if* they specifically state a substance abuse specialty. You can also go to the SAMHSA.gov Website, and look for "substance-abuse treatment." This will link you to your state and zip code. A competent substance-abuse professional can arrange for an assessment of your spouse or set up a professional intervention—a planned process that often leads the abuser to treatment.

Please note: if substance abuse is the problem affecting your family, it will not go away by itself. It is not your fault, and you can make a difference.

Relationship Firewalls

Barriers To Healthy Adult Attachments

By Margaret Meinecke, LCSW, CAC III & Forrest Lien, LCSW

Throughout history, humans have been interested in the stories of their predecessors and have learned from previous generations the problem solving skills necessary for survival. Like all animals, the young develop their abilities by modeling the behaviors of their elders. By their conscious, deliberate questioning and the less obvious mimicry of their parents and older siblings, children begin to understand and influence their environment.

Children look to their parents for safety and guidance as they experience emotional conflict. Children are seeking a secure foundation to develop an attachment schema for relationships. Without the secure base, children will develop a skill set of survival strategies for self protection and pain avoidance. Collected and practiced over time, the skill set developed will serve them although they may be quite unaware about its origin or development. This skill set or attachment schema becomes "hard-wired" over time and will be utilized when triggered by sadness and fear. Each of us brings an attachment skill set to the dance of relationship. When the relationship dance is fun and exciting, like in courtship, we don't need the survival skill set to avoid emotional pain.

Chris and Sue recently came to therapy because they were having communication problems. Sue was demanding and emotionally needy in her communication with Chris. Chris would check out or leave during these exchanges. Chris came from a childhood of several divorces and the death of his father at age five. He learned to numb out his feelings very early. Sue came from a family where her mother was dependent and needy and her father was cruel and controlling but gave Sue everything including material things. Both have been successful in business and friendship relationships but mean to each other after three years of marriage and two children. I attempted the traditional talk therapy approach of teaching them how to communicate better but he would always default to "emotionally checking out" and she would go on the attack. Their attachment styles that they learned from childhood were in active survival mode. The two most common feelings triggered for Chris and Sue was fear and sadness. When these feelings were triggered, their defenses went into action to protect them from those feelings. Adults with attachment difficulties want to be loved and accepted but don't have the "tools" to achieve that goal. Their cognitive distortions sabotage what they want and need.

When adults engage in attachment therapy to better understand their difficulties in relationships, they are helped with a number of clinical interventions designed to "re-wire" some of the cognitive circuitry that developed throughout their childhood. Thus the work with adults seeking a greater awareness of their emotional health and intimacy issues related to key relationships is two-fold. Clinical exploration to recall the feelings of self that developed throughout childhood is known as the emotional work. The examination of thoughts and ideas that evolved from early life experiences is known as cognitive work. By reviewing both feelings and thoughts, the adult engaged in therapy can then choose to challenge their system that lacks tools to effectively engage in satisfying emotionally intimate relationships.

Cognitive/emotional restructuring may include exercises such as life scripting wherein the family messages and habits of relating to others are closely examined and parents are discovered. Bringing into awareness the many subtle messages received in childhood and the thoughts and ideas developed from the family environment is often a first step toward changing the dysfunctional, and often unconscious, patterns of adulthood. Finding the origin of a faulty message, re-framing the message by understanding the limitations of the messenger(s) and practicing to incorporate a healthier, more accurate idea can be very liberating for a troubled adult operating from a painful or inconsistent set of childhood lessons.

Another clinical tool is legacy work in which a person is helped to examine the key relationships from which they have drawn life skills and information. In this work, an adult seeking understanding of their challenges will identify key persons from childhood, such as parents, caregivers, siblings, etc. and list character traits of those individuals. The list is then evaluated for the contributions from each person on the list to the skill set of the adult. Similarities are noted. The character trait list of the individual doing the work to understand his emotional "blueprint" is more readily available for exploration. Utilizing guided imagery, psycho dramatic role play, and EMDR allows the clinician to access the neurological pathways to childhood feelings. Often times we utilize these techniques while the client is being held by their partner as they explore the scary feelings of childhood. This posture promotes safety and physical connection.

When an adult engages in the clinical work of examining their use of the emotional and mental information from childhood, they bring into their control the choices associated with adult relationships and functioning. As their awareness grows, they gradually change the behaviors that do not support the healthy adult life they envision for themselves as members of their community, family and primary partnerships. Leaving the prisons of their past, they are freed into a world of possibilities where they can more fully and consciously enjoy their lives.

For more information please check our website at www.frlcounseling. com.

Kindle the Kids

by Francine Bianco Tax

My name if Francine Bianco Tax, and I have been the host and producer of the *Parenting Matters* radio program for over ten years. Through that venue, I have had the good fortune to interview many parenting experts and authors.

BE A MODEL OF JOY AND LOVE OF LIFE

I had Dr. Linda Miles as a guest on my show numerous times, and in the course of our conversations, she helped me to see how I was holding on to problems and needed to live more authentically and give my children a joyful, meaningful model of adulthood.

EXPRESS YOUR GIFTS AND PASSIONS

As new parents, we can easily lose ourselves in the responsibilities of care giving and forget to express our own gifts and passions.

Following the birth of my twins, I put my acting career on indefinite hold and was afraid to start again. Dr. Miles helped me kick through a wall of doubt, get focused, and formulate a realistic plan that honored me and my children.

BALANCE BEAM

I now have a balanced life as an actress in New York and a mom. My children see that I am following my dreams, and I believe that will help give them the courage to do this when they grow up. We are all better off.

My wish is to help others to lead the life that they want to model for their children. Life is complicated, messy, and challenging, but as you juggle your priorities, I wish for you a balanced, fulfilled life. And give your kids a hug for me.

Your Turn

Ask yourself the following questions:

- Are you able to face your problems, accept the pain, feel it, and let go so you can move on?
- Do you help your children express their feelings, then help guide them toward constructive solutions?
- Are you providing a healthy model of a fulfilled life as an adult? If not, what are some changes you can commit to make?
- Do you hold on to anger and bitterness, or do you know that *you* are the change?
- Does your model help empower your children to make changes?
- Are you able to use prayer and meditation to calm yourself and get centered?
- Are you able to discuss problems with your children without shame and blame?
- Do you trust your intuition?
- Can you connect with your children and utilize teachable moments?
- Do you celebrate life on a daily basis?
- Do you have a network to help support you as a parent?

Use these questions as a guide toward providing a terrific model for your kids.

Sizzling Senior Sex

By Dr. Shuford Davis

Kathryn and Stan are both seventy-eight and have been together for forty years. Over the years, they have enjoyed sexual contact in many ways.

EXCHANGE OF AFFECTION

This couple defines sex as an exchange of affection, so when Kathryn had breast cancer, they made adjustments and kept on keeping on.

At age seventy, Stan learned that he had prostate cancer, so they read up on medications for erectile dysfunction as well as natural supplements like yohimbine and arginine nitric oxide enhancer. They were determined to maintain a friendship on fire.

Sizzling Senior Sex (SSS) is a state of mind. You are never too old for sizzling sex. Masters and Johnson's research proved that couples were fully capable of enjoyable sexual activity into their eighties. SSS is always a matter of what's between your ears, not what's between your legs. If you think you are too old, your sizzle will fizzle. Think and believe, 'Yeah, baby!"

Sizzling senior sex summons individual sensitivity. Our bodies change over time. Talking about what is pleasurable and what is not is very important. In general, arousal is not as fast for either person or, for males, as instant as when you were thirty. SSS takes time and sensitivity. Enjoy the journey.

Sizzling senior sex counts on knowledge. Menopause changes many things for women. Husbands, go to her doctor's appointments, listen, become knowledgeable about the changes occurring in her body and emotions. If you are gentle and understanding with all this, she will be grateful. As men age, erections become less spontaneous and less firm. Television ads promote several medications for male enhancement. Both of you have to learn what happens to your body as you age. The good news is, growing old does not have to mean no sex. It may mean more lubricants, taking your pill, or changing to more comfortable positions. Think of it as not growing older but growing better.

Sizzling senior sex is increased the longer we stay healthy. Work out, find a hobby, keep your mind active, volunteer, and participate in religious activities. Research indicates all these activities promote aging well. Taking good care of yourself physically, mentally, and spiritually are key ingredients in staying healthy. If nature and genetics do not cooperate and physical challenges occur, remember attitude is everything: keeping positive keeps us alive.

Sizzling senior sex heats up in direct relationship to our happiness quotient. If you are an old fart, then you will stink up things and pizzle on your sizzle. Stay positive and upbeat, not dwelling on aches, pains, and illness. A positive, joyful, happy attitude will lift our spirit. Positive people believe everything is possible. Believe in great sex at any age. Let the sizzle begin!

Sizzling senior sex enjoys sensuality. If you always counted frequency of intercourse as the standard for good sex, you probably won't get this. So skip to number 7, or put your head in a blender. SSS enjoys a bath or shower together, sleeping bare, snuggling on the couch during an afternoon nap or holding hands on any walk. SSS begins with touch, not just doing it.

Sizzling senior sex says, "I love you." Making love is an extension of being in love. It's not the frequency, it's the passion. Long looks into each other's eyes, consciously doing things that please your spouse, planning a romantic evening put the sizzle into a senior marriage. After your passionate evening, bask in the afterglow and ask, "Wonder what the other geezers are doing tonight?" Then give thanks for SSS.

Your Turn

Review the principles in this article, and list ways you can apply the suggestions to your senior sex life.

Healing the Burns of Divorce

Dr. Amy Botwinick

Prince Charming has either turned into a toad or run off with Sleeping Beauty; now what?

Now what turns out to be the ultimate question when you start to look at divorce head-on? As I fumbled my way through the process, I felt desperate and uncertain. I was barely functioning as a result of my "divorce hangover."

BEFORE A DIVORCE

If you are contemplating divorce, the first thing you need is to get a reality check. The grass is not always greener. You'll avoid serious regret; you owe it to yourself and your family to take a good look at the realities of divorce now before moving forward. Be proactive and give it your best shot to avoid later remorse.

THE AFTER STAGE

If you ultimately divorce, you can learn to move on and take charge of your life. Evaluate your mistakes, take responsibility for destructive behavior, and begin to focus on your new life with a healthy perspective and sense of adventure.

Your Turn

You can use the experience of your divorce to your advantage or disadvantage. Your happily-ever-after depends on learning from your failed relationship as you work on creating new healthier ones. Don't let your bad experience with marriage leave you bitter and untrusting because then you really do lose.

Make a list of the lessons that you have learned from divorce or relationship strife, and commit yourself to change.

Dr. Amy can be reached for consultation at dramy@womenmovingon.com.

The Shooting Star, Rece

by Jinmi and Nick Huseman

Rece Nicholas Huseman was like a shooting star that burned briefly and brightly in the lives of his parents. When he died from Sudden Infant Death Syndrome (SIDS) at seven months, this young couple faced one of life's greatest hardships—the loss of a child. Their description of coping with this loss is a beautiful example of friendship on fire.

Jinmi writes, "Our love for one another is what brought Rece into this world. We understand each other more than anyone else does. We may grieve differently, but we both lost the most important person in our lives . . . Rece. The greatest tribute to Rece is to show each other the love that he has brought into our lives."

COMMON GROUND

It is difficult to put our egos aside in the midst of an argument when emotions are charged. We have to stop and ask ourselves what is really important. Is it winning an argument or finding common ground where we can really see each other? There is no blame around losing Rece.

LIVING IN THE MOMENT

The love bond with a child is the strongest and most sacred one in the universe. The pain of the loss is equal to the love. We have learned to use meditation to deal with the pain. When Rece passed, surviving became matter of getting through each minute, and meditation taught us to live in the moment rather than through it. I also write to Rece in my journal.

EXPOSE RAW EMOTION

What has held us together is the willingness to allow ourselves to expose our raw emotions. We allow each other to grieve to our own pace without judging one another. I remember collapsing in the middle of the room in a sobbing fit, and Nick took me to bed, looked into my eyes, and told how much he loves me.

ETERNAL SOUL

What is most important is to have faith that Rece is OK. We believe our love bonds will keep us together forever. Each of us has an eternal soul that binds us to the people we love forever.

Twenty-Six Conclusions

from Why Marriage Matters, Second Edition.
A report from Family Scholars 2005.
The Institute for American Values

Family

1. Marriage increases the likelihood that fathers and mothers have good relationships with their children.
2. Cohabitation is not the functional equivalent of marriage.
3. Growing up outside an intact marriage increases the likelihood that children will themselves divorce or become unwed parents.
4. Marriage is a virtually universal human institution.
5. Marriage and a normative commitment to marriage, foster high quality relationships between adults, as well as between parents and children.
6. Marriage has important biosocial consequences for adults and children.

Economics

7. Divorce and unmarried childbearing increase poverty for both children and mothers.
8. Married couples seem to build more wealth on average than single or cohabiting couples.

9. Marriage reduces poverty and material hardship for disadvantaged women and their children.
10. Minorities benefit economically from marriage.
11. Married man and more money than do single men with similar education and job histories.
12. Parental divorce (or failure to marry) appears to increase children's risk of school failure.
13. Parental divorce reduces the likelihood that children will graduate from college and achieve high status jobs.

Physical health and longevity

14. Children who live with their own two married parents enjoy better physical health, on average, than do children and other family forms.
15. Parental marriage is associated with a sharply lower risk of infant mortality.
16. Marriage is associated with reduced rates of alcohol and substance abuse for both adults and teens.
17. Married people, especially married men, have longer life expectancies than do otherwise similar singles
18. Marriage is associated with better health and lower rates of injury, illness, and disability for both men and women.
19. Marriage seems to be associated with better health among minorities and the poor.

Mental health and emotional well-being.

20. Children whose parents divorce have higher rates of psychological distress and mental illness.
21. Divorce appears to increase significantly the risk of suicide.
22. Married mothers have lower rates of depression than do single or cohabiting mothers.
23. Boys raised in single-parent families are more likely to engage in delinquent and criminal behavior.
24. Marriage appears to reduce the risk that adults will beat either perpetrators or victims of crime.

25. Married women appear to have a lower risk of experiencing domestic violence than to cohabiting or dating women.
26. A child who is not living with his or her own two married parents is at greater risk for child abuse.

CLOSING THOUGHTS

I hope this book illuminated for you what it means to sustain a friendship on fire. If you do not foster a sense of safety, a deep and abiding connection, and one another's unique spirits, you may find yourself with an uncontrolled burn on your hands.

Even if you find yourself relating to a lot of the questionnaire questions, don't worry. These all represent common relationship problems. With work and a lot of love, the two of you can build a more supportive and empathetic relationship. Once you get out of your own way by shutting off those pesky ego tapes, ignoring toxic thought patterns, retraining your brain, and learning true relaxation techniques, you will be well on the way to a friendship on fire.

APPENDIX

Appendix

Questionnaire Questions & Related "Your Turn" Exercises

Every relationship is unique and, therefore, comes with its own unique set of problems. Use this handy page reference guide to locate the sections and exercises that tackle the specific issues you and your partner acknowledged in the questionnaire.

Question	Section Page #s	Your Turn Page #s
1. I feel isolated and lonely.	31, 32, 39, 44-45, 49-53, 59, 65-67, 70-71, 88-89, 109, 112-114, 128-130, 144-145, 155-156, 167, 169-170, 180, 186-188	40, 54-55, 66, 68-69, 77-78, 80-81, 83-84, 90-91, 92-96, 114-115, 120, 130, 142-143, 146, 156-157, 170-171, 178-179, 207
2. I am intolerant of my partner.	41-45, 43, 50, 56, 57, 76-77, 82-83, 86, 99-100, 107, 112-114, 119-120, 121-123, 124, 128-130, 135-136, 147-149, 158-160, 165-166, 172-173, 178, 186-188, 198-200	43-44, 47-48, 54-55, 58, 66, 68-69, 80-81, 86-87, 90-91, 92-96, 114-115, 120, 130, 136, 139, 142-143, 159, 173-174, 184-185

3. I resent my partner.	41-42, 44-45, 46-47, 50, 56, 57, 60, 82-83, 86, 99-100, 107,112-114,119-120,121-123,124,128-130,135-136, 137-139,140-141,147-149, 158-160,165-166,169-170, 172-173,178,182-184,186-188,198-200	43-44, 47-48, 54-55, 58, 66, 68-69, 77-78, 80-81, 86-87, 90-91, 92-96, 114-115, 120, 130, 136, 139, 142-143, 159, 173-174, 184-185, 202
4. I lash out at my partner.	41-47, 57, 60, 86, 99-100, 112-114, 119-120, 121-123, 124, 135-136, 141, 158-160, 165-166, 172-173, 182-184, 186-188, 198-200	43-44, 47-48, 54-55, 58, 61, 68-69, 86-87, 92-96, 120, 123-124, 136, 142-143, 159, 173-174, 184-185
5. My partner lashes out at me.	41-47, 57, 60, 86, 99-100, 109, 119-120, 121-123, 124, 135-136, 141, 158-160, 165-166, 172-173, 182-184,186-188,198-200	43-44, 47-48, 54-55, 58, 61, 68-69, 86-87, 92-96, 120, 123-124, 136, 142-143, 159, 173-174, 184-185
6.Sex is a major problem for us.	42, 68, 102-104, 144-145, 180, 186-188, 203-205	92-96, 105, 114-115, 146, 205
7. I use criticism too often.	41-45, 50, 56, 57, 60, 76-77, 86, 99-100, 121-123, 124, 135-136, 140-141, 158-160, 165-166, 172-173, 182-184, 186-188, 198-200	43-44, 47-48, 54-55, 58, 61, 68-69, 86-87, 92-96, 114-115, 120, 123-124, 130, 136, 142-143, 159, 173-174, 184-185
8. My partner uses criticism too often.	41-45, 56, 57, 60, 86, 99-100, 119-120, 121-123, 124, 135-136, 140-141, 158-160,165-166,172-173, 182-184,186-188,198-200	43-44, 47-48, 54-55, 58, 61, 68-69, 86-87, 92-96, 114-115, 120, 123-124, 130, 136, 159, 173-174, 184-185
9. I have lost respect for my partner.	41-47, 56, 57, 76-77, 82-83, 86, 99-100, 112-114, 119-120, 128-130, 135-136, 147-149, 158-160, 165-166, 172-173, 182-184, 186-188, 198-200	43-44, 47-48, 54-55, 58, 66, 68-69, 80-81, 86-87, 90-91, 92-96, 114-115, 120, 130, 136, 142-143, 159, 173-174, 184-185, 202

10. My partner has lost respect for me.	41-45, 56, 57, 82-83, 86, 99-100, 112-114, 119-120, 135-136, 147-149, 158-160, 165-166, 172-173, 178, 182-184, 186-188, 198-200	43-44, 47-48, 54-55, 58, 66, 68-69, 80-81, 86-87, 90-91, 92-96, 114-115, 120, 130, 136, 159, 173-174, 184-185, 202
11. We avoid dealing with conflicts.	41-43, 46-47, 86, 99-100, 112-114, 135-136, 137-139, 140-141, 172-173, 178, 186-188, 198-200	47-48, 68-69, 80-81, 83-84, 86-87, 92-96, 136, 139, 173-174, 184-185, 202
12. We need to learn how to fight fair.	41-47, 57, 60, 86, 99-100, 119-120, 121-123, 124, 135-136, 137-139, 141, 165-166, 172-173, 182-184, 186-188, 198-200	43-44, 47-48, 58, 61, 68-69, 80-81, 86-87, 92-96, 114-115, 120, 123-124, 130, 136, 159, 173-174, 184-185, 202
13. Our life together is boring.	36-37, 42, 73-74, 99-100, 102-104, 116-117, 131-133, 161, 186-188	40, 68-69, 77-78, 92-96, 105, 114-115, 117-118, 133-134, 146, 205
14. My life is too stressful.	35, 38-41, 44-45, 52-53, 61-62, 72, 109, 175-176, 189-194	58, 92-96, 110-111, 161-162, 168, 176-177, 202
15. I experience very little joy.	32, 36-37, 49, 52-54, 61-62, 70-71, 72, 79-80, 83, 89, 99-100, 102-104, 109, 116-117, 131-133, 155-156, 161, 166-167, 175-176	40, 58, 61, 83-84, 92-96, 105, 110-111, 114-115, 117-118, 133-134, 142-143, 146, 156-157, 161-162, 168, 176-177, 173-174, 178-179, 202, 205
16. I feel as if I have lost track of who I am.	32, 35-37, 40-41, 49, 51-52, 53-54, 65, 71-72, 77, 82-83, 88-89, 91, 118, 155-156, 166-167, 169-170	54-55, 58, 66, 80-81, 83-84, 92-96, 110-111, 142-143, 156-157, 161-162, 168, 170-171, 178-179, 181, 202
17. I have recently experienced a death in the immediate family.	31-33, 208-209	92-96
18. I feel anxious a lot.	34, 35, 38-40, 44-45, 52-53, 61-62, 65-67, 70-72, 161, 175-176	58, 61, 92-96, 110-111, 161-162, 168, 170-171, 173-174, 176-177, 202

19. I feel a sense of emptiness.	32, 35-37, 39, 44-45, 51-54, 61-62, 65-67, 70-71, 79-80, 82-83, 89, 109, 118, 131-133, 155-156, 166-167, 175-176	54-55, 58, 83-84, 90-91, 92-96, 110-111, 114-115, 156-157, 161-162, 168, 178-179, 181, 202
20. I wish I could laugh more often.	65-67, 72, 116-117, 131-133, 144-145, 155-156, 175-176	54-55, 58, 92-96, 105, 110-111, 117-118, 156-157, 161-162, 168, 176-177
21. We do not work well as a team.	31, 39, 41-45, 50, 56, 57, 60, 76, 82-83, 86, 99-100, 109, 112-114, 119-120, 121-123, 124, 128-130, 135-136, 137-139, 140-142, 147-149, 158-161, 165-166, 169-170, 172-173, 178, 182-184, 186-188, 198-200, 201-202	40, 43-44, 58, 68-69, 80-81, 83-84, 86-87, 92-96, 105, 114-115, 120, 130, 136, 139, 149, 159, 164, 173-174, 176-177, 184-185, 202
22. We do not support one another when we are dealing with the children.	31, 44-45, 56, 119-120, 125-126, 178, 186-188, 198-200, 201-202, 208-209	43-44, 58, 80-81, 86-87, 92-96, 120, 127, 142-143, 159, 176-177, 202
23. I experience a lack of purpose in my life.	32, 36-37, 39, 49, 51-52, 65-67, 70, 72, 79-80, 155-156	54-55, 58, 80-81, 83-84, 90-91, 92-96, 110-111, 161-162, 168, 181, 202
24. I worry a lot.	32, 34, 35, 38-40, 44-45, 52-53, 61-62, 65-67, 72, 161, 175-176	58, 61, 92-96, 110-111, 161-162, 168, 176-177, 202
25. My partner and I have lost our connection.	31, 32, 36-37, 39, 41-42, 44-47, 56, 57, 65, 68, 73-74, 82-83, 102-104, 109-110, 112-114, 116-117, 118, 128-130, 131-133, 137-139, 140-142, 144-145, 147-149, 163-164, 169-170, 172-173, 182-184, 186-188, 189-194, 198-200, 208-209	40, 43-44, 47-48, 54-55, 58, 66, 68-69, 77-78, 80-81, 83-84, 92-96, 105, 114-115, 117-118, 120, 130, 133-134, 139, 146, 149, 159, 164, 173-174, 176-177, 184-185, 194, 205

26. We have a hard time understanding one another.	36-37, 39, 41, 43, 44-45, 57, 68, 73-74, 82-83, 86, 109-110, 112-114, 119, 128-130, 135-136, 137-139, 140-142, 147-149, 169-170, 182-184, 186-188, 189-194, 198-200, 208-209	40, 43-44, 54-55, 58, 66, 68-69, 77-78, 80-81, 83-84, 92-96, 114-115, 120, 136, 139, 149, 159, 164, 173-174, 184-185, 194
27. I have lost trust in my partner.	41-43, 56, 99-100, 135-136, 141-142, 172-173, 182-184, 186-188, 198-200	43-44, 66, 68-69, 80-81, 136, 159, 173-174, 184-185
28. My partner has lost trust in me.	41-43, 56, 99-100, 135-136, 141-142, 172-173, 182-184, 186-188, 198-200	43-44, 66, 68-69, 80-81, 136, 159, 173-174, 184-185
29. I keep my unhappiness inside and pretend that things are OK.	32, 46-47, 66-67, 70, 72, 79-80, 155-156, 169-170, 175-176	47-48, 68-69, 80-81, 83-84, 92-96, 110-111, 114-115, 156-157, 161-162, 170-171, 173-174
30. I have felt depressed for more than a month.	66-67, 72, 155-156, 166-167, 175-176	92-96, 110-111, 156-157
31. I have a problem with drinking or drugs.	71, 72, 195-196	72, 92-96, 196-197
32. My partner has a problem with drinking or drugs.	71, 72, 195-196	72, 92-96, 196-197
33. I put myself down too much.	32, 34, 36-37, 39-41, 44-45, 49, 50-52, 65, 70-71, 107, 155-156, 158, 169-170	54-55, 92-96, 110-111, 156-157, 170-171, 181
34. I feel like I always have to be the grown-up.	41-45, 49, 99-100, 124, 186-188	43-44, 54-55, 66, 68-69, 80-81, 92-96, 110-111, 114-115, 176-177
35. I wish we had a spiritual practice.	32, 35-36, 44-45, 52-53, 61-62, 66-67, 72, 110, 118	90-91, 173-174, 202

Bibliography

Arrien, Angeles. *The Second Half of Life*. Boulder: Sounds True, 2005.

Austin, James H., M.D. *Zen and the Brain*. Cambridge, MA: The MIT Press, 1998.

Brach, Tara. *Radical Acceptance*. New York: Bantam Books, 2003.

Brockrnan, Richard, M.D. *A Map of the Mind toward a Science of Psychotherapy*. Madison. Connecticut: Psychosocial Press, 1998.

Brussat, Frederic and Mary Ann Brussat. *Spiritual Literacy*. New York: Touchstone, 1996.

Carter, Rita. *Mapping the Mind*. Berkeley: University of California Press, 1999.

Chödrön, Pema. *Good Medicine*. Boulder: Sounds True DVD, 2007.

Claypool, John. *God: The Ingenious Alchemist*. London: Morehouse Publishing, 2005.

Damassio, Antonio. *The Feeling of What Happens*. San Diego: Harcourt, Inc., 1999.

Davidson, Richard J. and Jon Kabat-Zinn. "Alterations in Brain and Immune Functions Produced by Mindfulness Meditation: Three Caveats." *Psychosomatic Medicine* 2004: 66:148-152.

Drevets, Wayne. "Decade of Work Shows Depression is Physical." *JAMA* 10 April 2002.

Goleman, Daniel. *Emotional Intelligence*. New York: Bantam Books, 1995.

Ekman, Paul. *Emotions Revealed*. New York: Henry Holt & Company, 2004.

Ekman, Paul and Erika L. Rosenberg, eds. *What the Face Reveals*. New York: Oxford University Press, 2005.

Fisher, Helen. *Why We Love*. New York: Henry Holt and Company, 2004.

Goldberg, Elkhonon. *The Executive Brain*. Oxford: Oxford University Press, 2001.

Goleman, Daniel. *Social Intelligence*. New York: Bantam Books, 2006.

Gottman, John M. *Why Marriages Succeed or Fail*. New York: Simon and Schuster, 1994.

Gottman, John M. and Nan Silver. *The Seven Principles for Making Marriage Work*. New York: Crown Publishing Incorporated, 1999.

Greenfield, Susan A. *The Private Life of the Brain*. New York: John Wiley and Sons, Inc., 2001.

Hayes, Stephen and Spencer Smith. *Get Out of Your Mind and Into Your Life*. Oakland: New Harbinger Publications, 2005.

Hendricks, Harville. *Getting The Love You Want: A Guide for Couples*. New York: Henry Holt and Company, 1988.

Johnson, Dr. Sue. *Hold Me Tight: Seven Conversations for a Lifetime of Love*. New York: Little, Brown and Company, 2008.

Jung. C.G. *Analytical Psychology: Its Theory and Practice: The Tavistock Lectures*. New York: Pantheon Books, 1968.

Jung, C.G. *The Archetypes and the Collective Unconscious*. Trans. R.F.C. Hull. Princeton: Princeton University Press, 1959.

Jung. C.G. *Dreams*. Trans. R.F.C. Hull. Princeton: Princeton University Press, 1974.

Jung. C.G. *Man and His Symbols*. Garden City, New York: Doubleday, 1964.

Jung. C.G. *Memories, Dreams, Reflections*. Aniela Jaffe, ed. London: Collins Fontana Library, 1967.

Jung, C.G. *Portable Jung*. Joseph Campbell, ed. New York: Viking Press, 1971.

Kabat-Zinn, Jon. *Arriving at Your Own Door*. New York: Hyperion, 2007.

Kabat-Zinn, Jon. *Coming to Our Senses: Healing Ourselves and the World Through Mindfulness*. New York: Hyperion Press, 2003.

Kabat-Zinn, Jon, Ph.D. *Full Catastrophe Living: Using the Wisdom of Your Body and Mind to Face Stress, Pain, and Illness*. New York: Dell 1990.

Kandel, E.R. "Genes, nerve cells, and the remembrance of things past." *The Journal of Neuropsychiatry* 1989. 1:103-25.

Kandel, E.R, James H. Schwartz, and Thomas M. Jessell. *Principles of Neural Science*. 3rd ed. New York: Elsevier Publishing, 1991.

Keating, Thomas. *Cloud of Unknowing*. Boulder: Sounds True CD, 2008.

Keating, Thomas. "Centering Prayer."

Kieves, Tama. *This Time I Dance: Creating the Work You Love*. Tarcher, 2006

Hazelden Foundation. *Keep it Simple*. Hazelden Foundation, 1989.

Lazarus, Richard S. *Psychological Stress and the Coping Process*. New York: McGraw Hill, 1966.

LeDoux, Joseph. *The Emotional Brain*. New York: Simon and Schuster, 1996.

LeDoux, Joseph. "Emotion and the Limbic System Concept." *Concepts in Neuroscience 2* 1991. 2:169-99.

Merton, Thomas. *New Seeds of Contemplation*. New York: New Directions, 1949.

Merton, Thomas. *Zen and the Birds of Appetite*. New York: New Directions, 1968.

Miles, Linda and Robert Miles. *The New Marriage: Transcending the Happily-Ever-After Myth*. Cypress House, 2000.

Miller, Alice. *The Drama of the Gifted Child: The Search for the True Self*. Trans. Ruth Ward. New York: Basic Books, 1994.

Moore, Thomas. *Care of the Soul: A Guide for Cultivating Depth and Sacredness in Everyday Life*. New York: Harper Collins, 1992.

Moore, Thomas. *Soul Mates: Honoring the Mysteries of Love and Relationship*. New York: Harper Collins Publishers, 1994.

Norris, Kathleen. *The Cloister Walk*. New York: Riverhead Books, 1996.

Nouwen, Henri. *The Return of "The Prodigal Son"*. New York: Image Books, 1992.

Papero, Daniel V. *Bowen Family Systems Theory*. Boston: Allyn and Bacon, 1990.

Pearson, Carol. *Awakening the Heroes*. San Francisco: Harper, 1991.

Polk, William R. *Polk's Folly: An American Family History*. New York: Doubleday, 2000.

Rilke, Rainer Maria. *Letters to a Young Poet*. Trans. M. D. Herter. New York: W.W. Norton, 1934.

Ryle, Anthony. *Frames and Cages: The Repertory Grid Approach to Human Understanding*. London: Sussex University Press, 1975.

Ryle, Anthony. *Neurosis in the Ordinary Family: A Psychiatric Survey*. London: Tavistock Publications, 1967.

Schnarch. David Morris. *Passionate Marriage: Love, Sex, and Intimacy in Emotionally Committed Relationships*. New York: W.W. Norton, 1997.

Seligman, Martin E.P., Ph.D. *Authentic Happiness: Using the New Positive Psychology to Realize Your Potential for Lasting Fulfillment.* New York: Free Press, 2003.

Sharp, Daryl. *Jung Lexicon: A Primer of Terms and Concepts.* Toronto, Canada: Inner City Books, 1991.

Siegel, Daniel J. *The Developing Mind: How Relationships and the Brain Interact to Shape Who We Are.* New York: Guilford Press, 2001.

Siegel, Daniel J. *The Mindful Brain.* New York: W.W. Norton and Company, Inc., 2007.

Spitz, René A. and W. Godfrey Cobliner. *The First Year of Life: A Psychoanalytic Study of Normal and Deviant Development of Object Relations.* New York: International Universities Press, 1965.

Sullivan, Harry Stack. *Personal Psychopathology: Early Formulations.* New York: Norton, 1953.

Sullivan, Harry Stack. *The Interpersonal Theory of Psychiatry.* Helen Swick Perry and Mary Ladd Gawel, eds. New York: Norton, 1953.

Thomas, Nancy. *When Love Is Not Enough.* Families by Design, 1997. (Contact at: P.O. Box 2812, Glenwood Springs, CO 81602.)

Tolle, Eckhart. *A New Earth: Awakening to Your Life's Purpose.* New York: Penguin Group, 2005.

Vanderwall, Francis. *Freedom from Fear: A Way through the Ways of Jesus the Christ.* Trent Angers, ed. Lafayette, Louisiana: Acadian House, 1999.

Vaughan, Frances E., Ph.D., and Roger N. Walsh, Ph.D., eds. *Accept This Gift: Selections from a Course in Miracles.* Los Angeles: J. P. Tarcher, 1992.

Wile, Daniel B. *Couples Therapy.* New York: Wiley, 1993.

Woodman, Marion. *The Pregnant Virgin: A Process of Psychological Transformation.* Toronto: Inner City Books, 1985.

Yeats, William Butler. *Selected Poems and Two Plays.* M.L. Rosenthal, ed. New York, Macmillan, 1962.

Zona, Guy. *The House of the Heart Is Never Full.* New York: Touchstone, 1993.

Index

I

imagery 40, 63-5, 82, 129, 133, 143
imagery guided 40, 200
inadequacy 50, 70, 99, 156, 191
intentions 14, 23, 28, 32, 37, 53-5, 61,
  88-91, 111, 114, 145
intimacy 71, 79, 102-3
intimacy canvas 102-3
intimidation 6, 100, 121, 123
intimidation tactics 121, 123-4

J

Jacobson, Edmund 40
Jampolsky, Gerald 104
Johnson, Samuel 23
journal 83, 90-5, 174, 176, 209
  relationship 92-3
journalizing 94-6
journey, spiritual 31, 33
judgment 35, 50, 62, 99, 111, 118-9,
  156, 158-9, 167, 169-71

K

Keating, Thomas 37
Kieves, Tama 136, 168
kiss 104, 143, 145
knowledge 14, 23, 80, 204

L

laughter 22, 102, 114, 116-7, 163
Lawrence 173
Lawrence, D. H. 173
leadership 126, 139, 164, 179
LeDoux, Joseph 133
lessons 16, 19, 25, 40, 50, 57, 60-1, 87,
  93-5, 139, 149, 194, 207
Lewis. C. S. 74
list 77, 95, 135-6, 158-9, 178, 205
list risk 77
love bonds 208-9
loving kindness 36, 52, 56-8, 62, 67, 86,
  123, 127, 148

M

magazine 82, 104, 132
male enhancement medication 203-4
marriage 15, 26, 33, 74, 88, 120, 128,
  132, 142, 164, 192, 205, 207
mask 71, 82, 137
mastectomy 189-90, 192
Masters and Johnson (research team)
  103, 203
meditation 16, 202, 208-9
memories 129, 141, 175, 183
menopause 204
mind, conscious 89
mind traps 109-11
Mindful Brain, The (Siegel, Dan) 109
mindfulness 111, 141, 156, 167, 222
mindfulness practice 51, 66, 111, 113-4,
  118, 141, 143, 156, 159, 167
mindfulness techniques 105
mistakes 5, 25, 38, 40, 42, 44, 52, 60, 68,
  79, 81, 96, 107, 136, 206
model 32, 73-4, 82, 102, 104, 127, 132,
  137, 142, 144, 146, 164, 193, 195,
  201-2
Moody, Raymond 118
Mother Teresa 57, 176, 190
"my way or the highway" verbiage 130

N

name-calling 160
Nar-Anon 196
near-death experience 118
negative belief systems 142
negative moods 161, 176
negative programming 51
negative thoughts 36, 44, 122, 155, 166
neural pathways 110
neurons 109-10, 148-9
  mirror 110, 148-9
neurons motor 148
neurotransmitters 166

O

P

R

S

Y

Printed in the United States
136364LV00002B/152/P